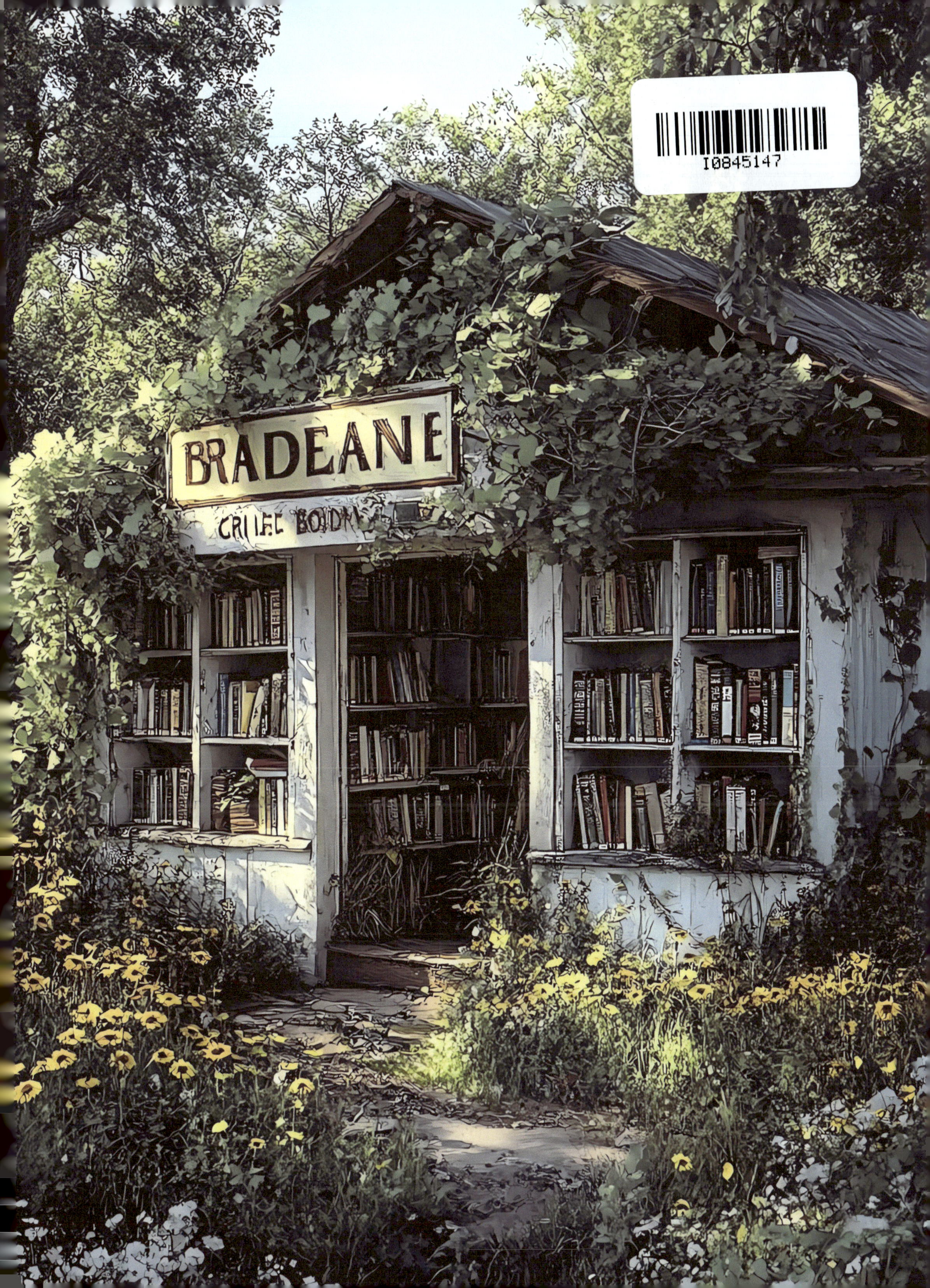

BRADEANE

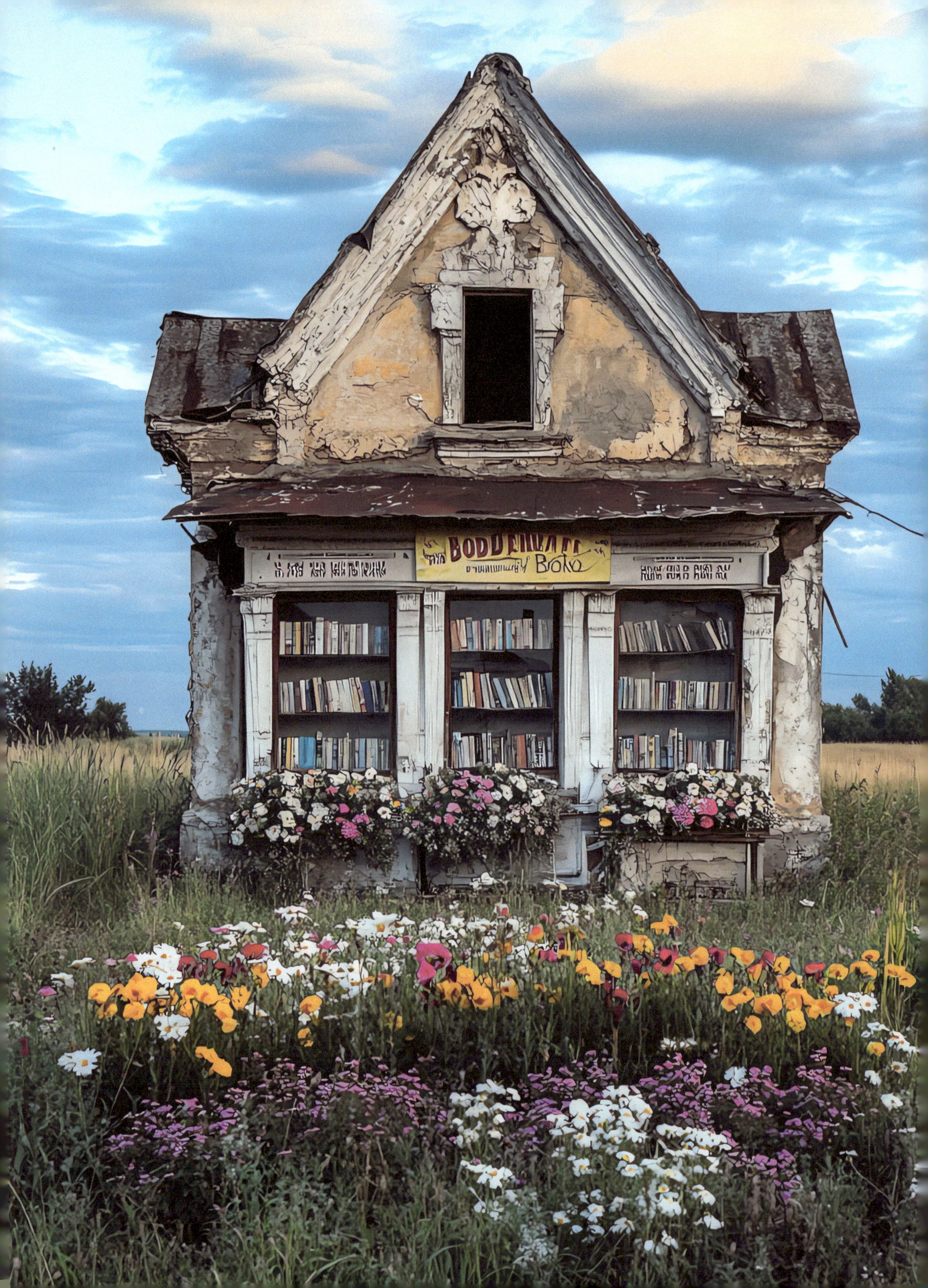
Books

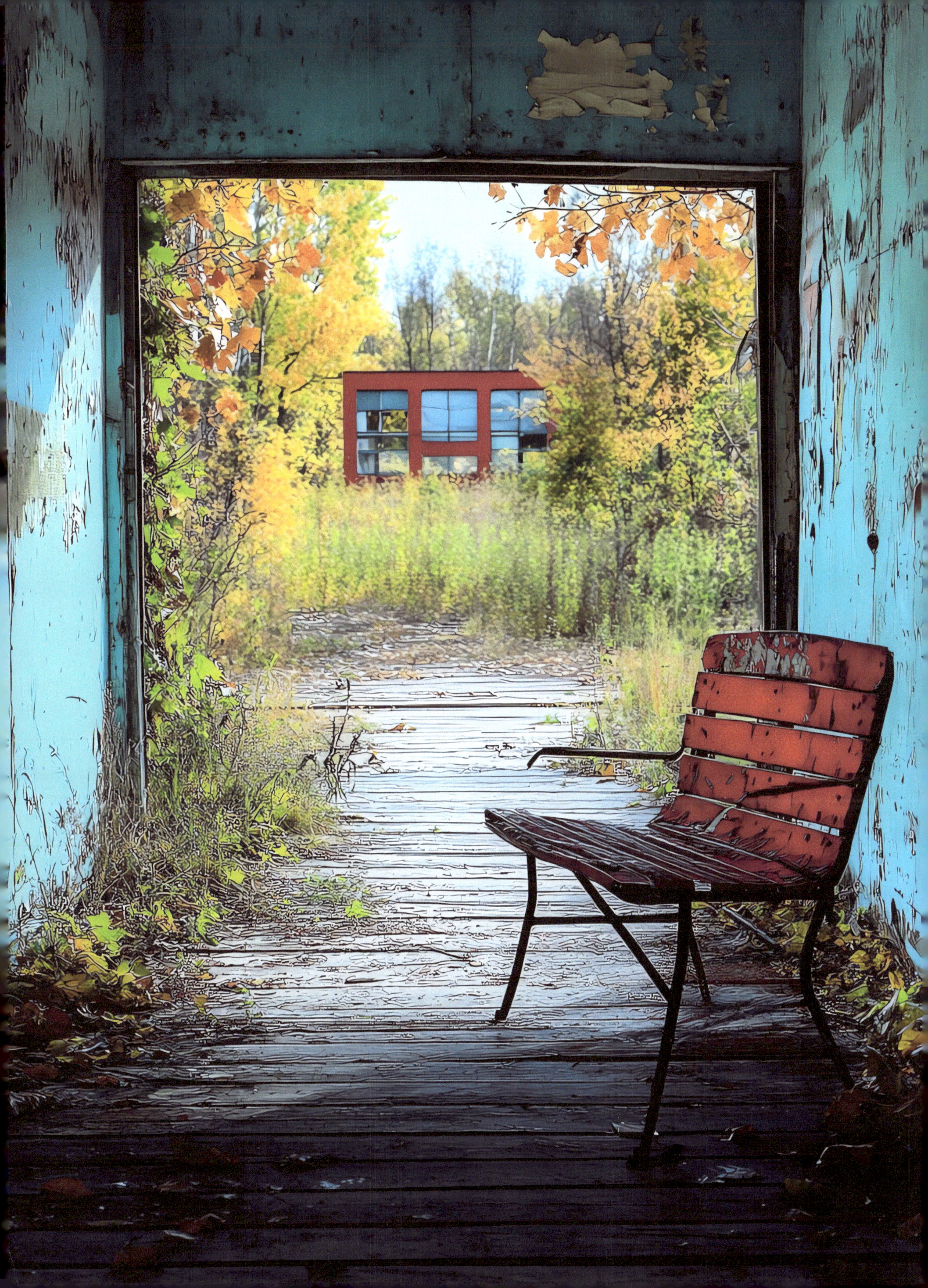

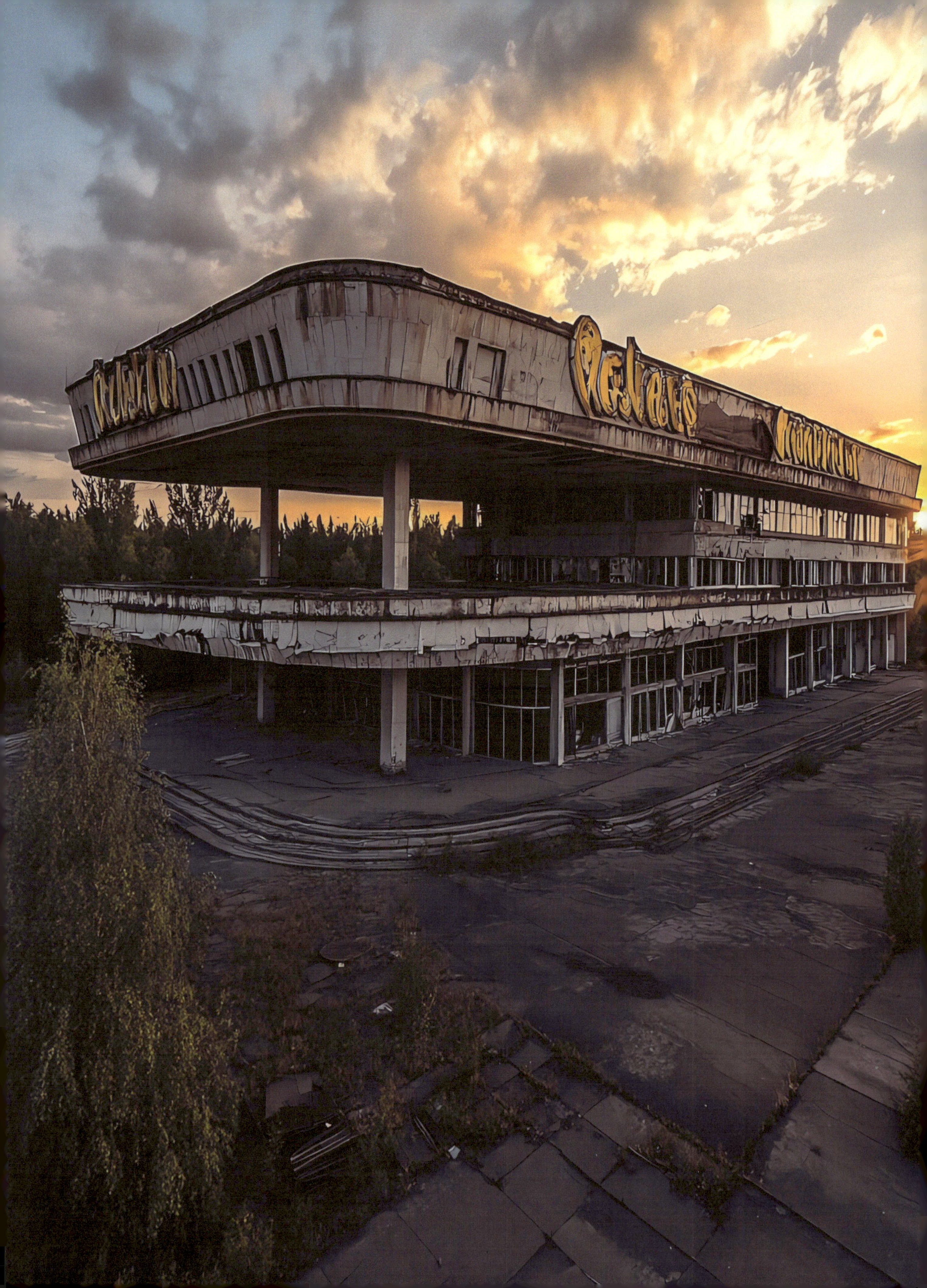

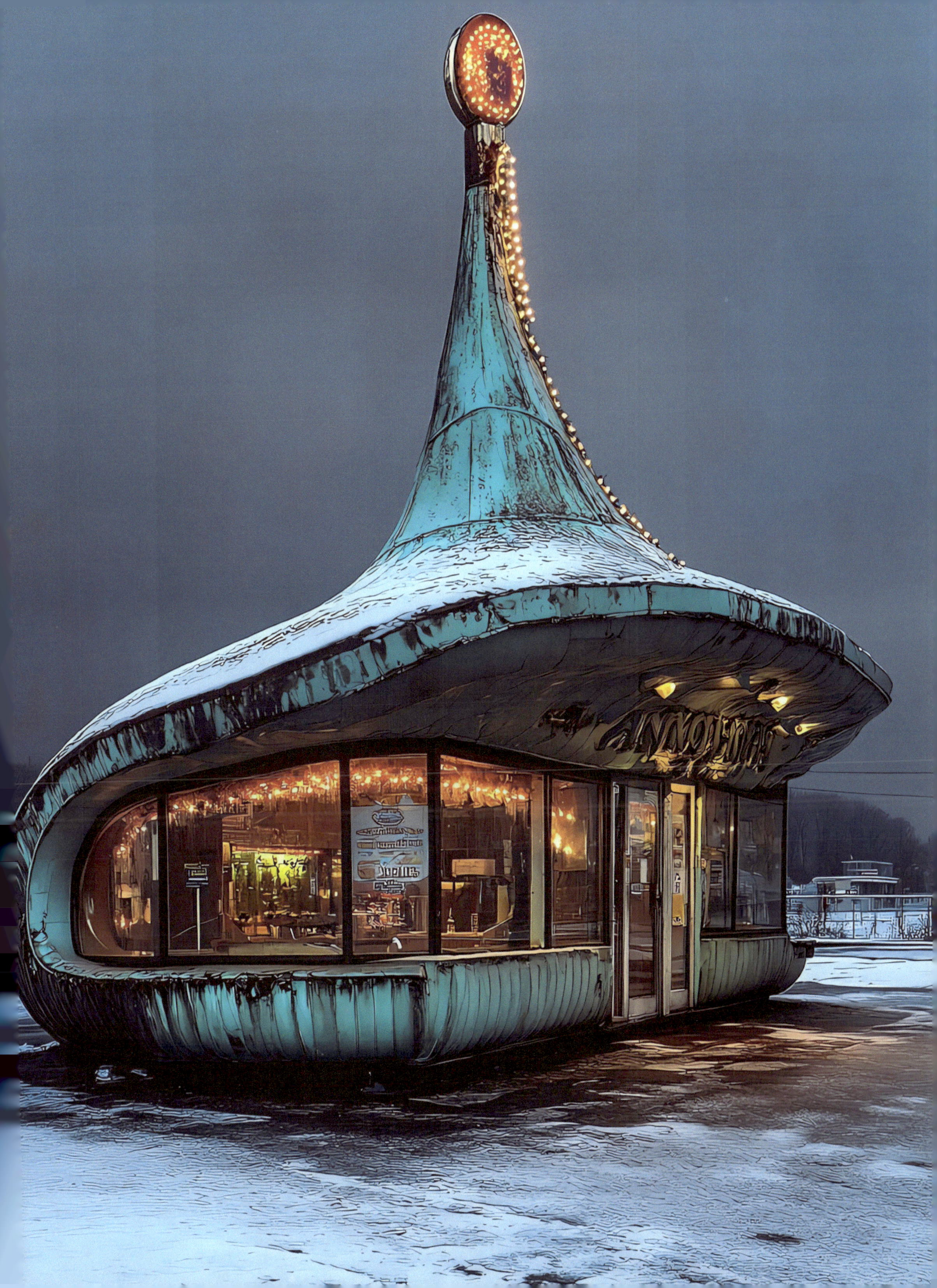

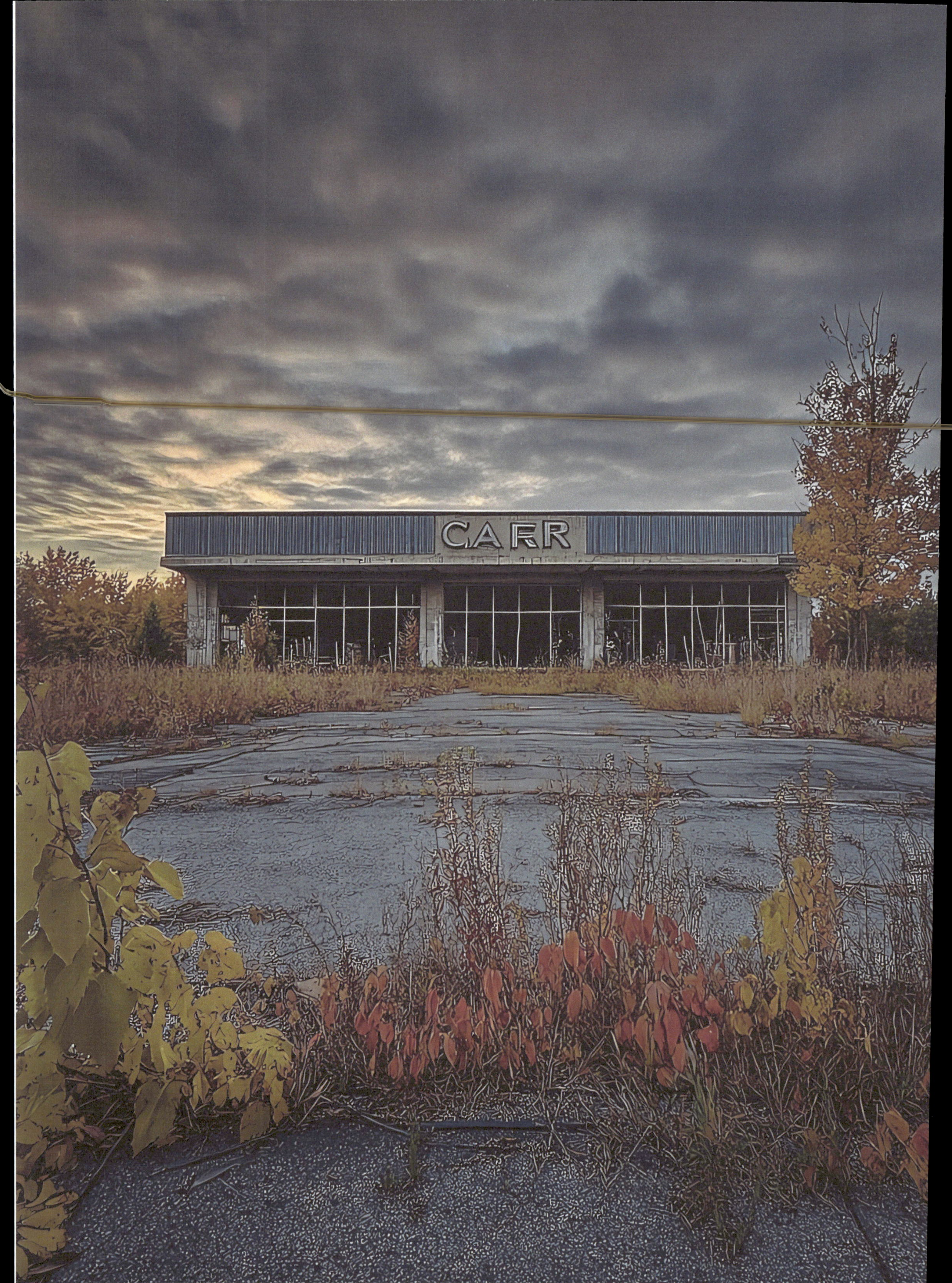

CARR

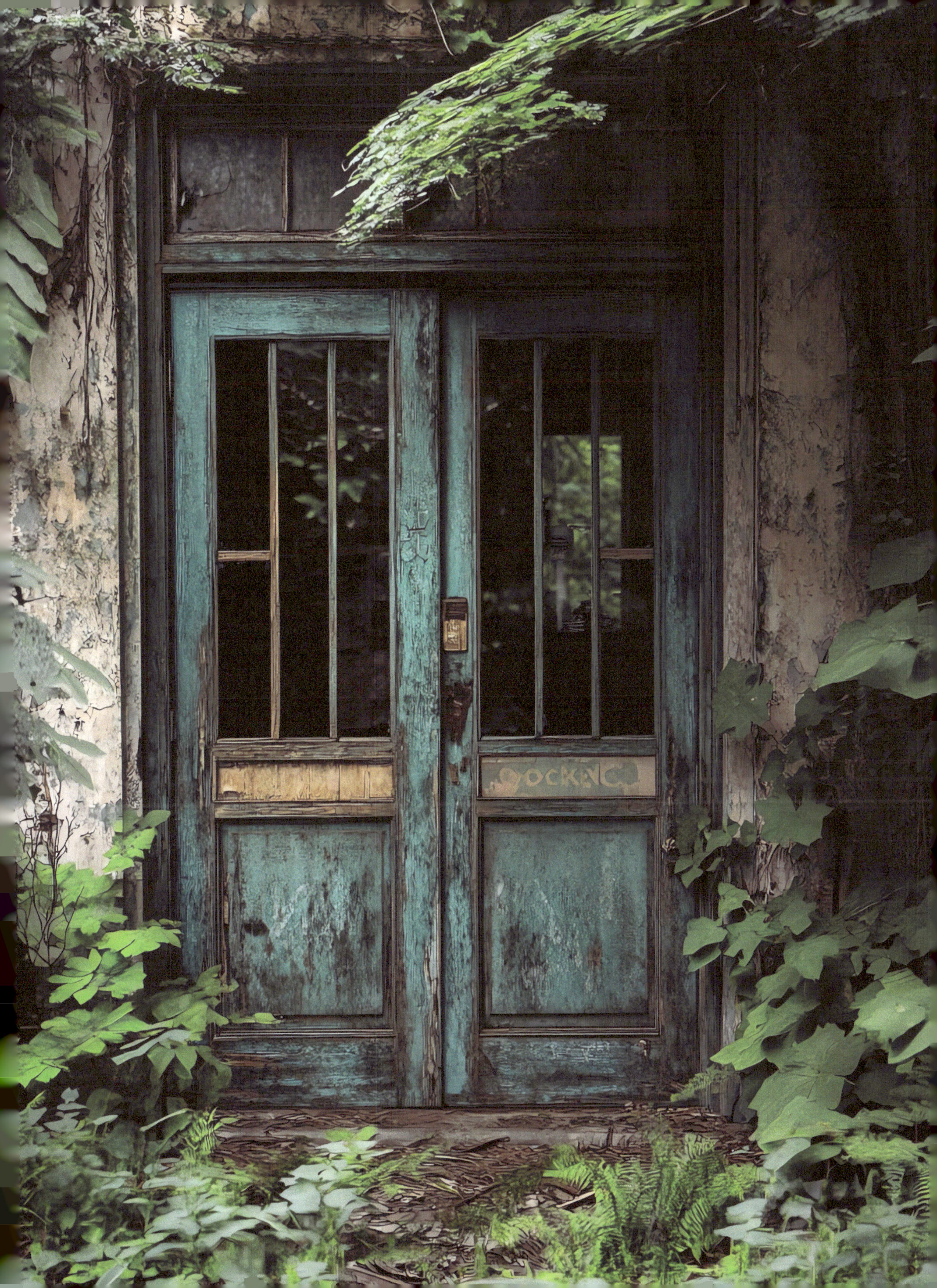

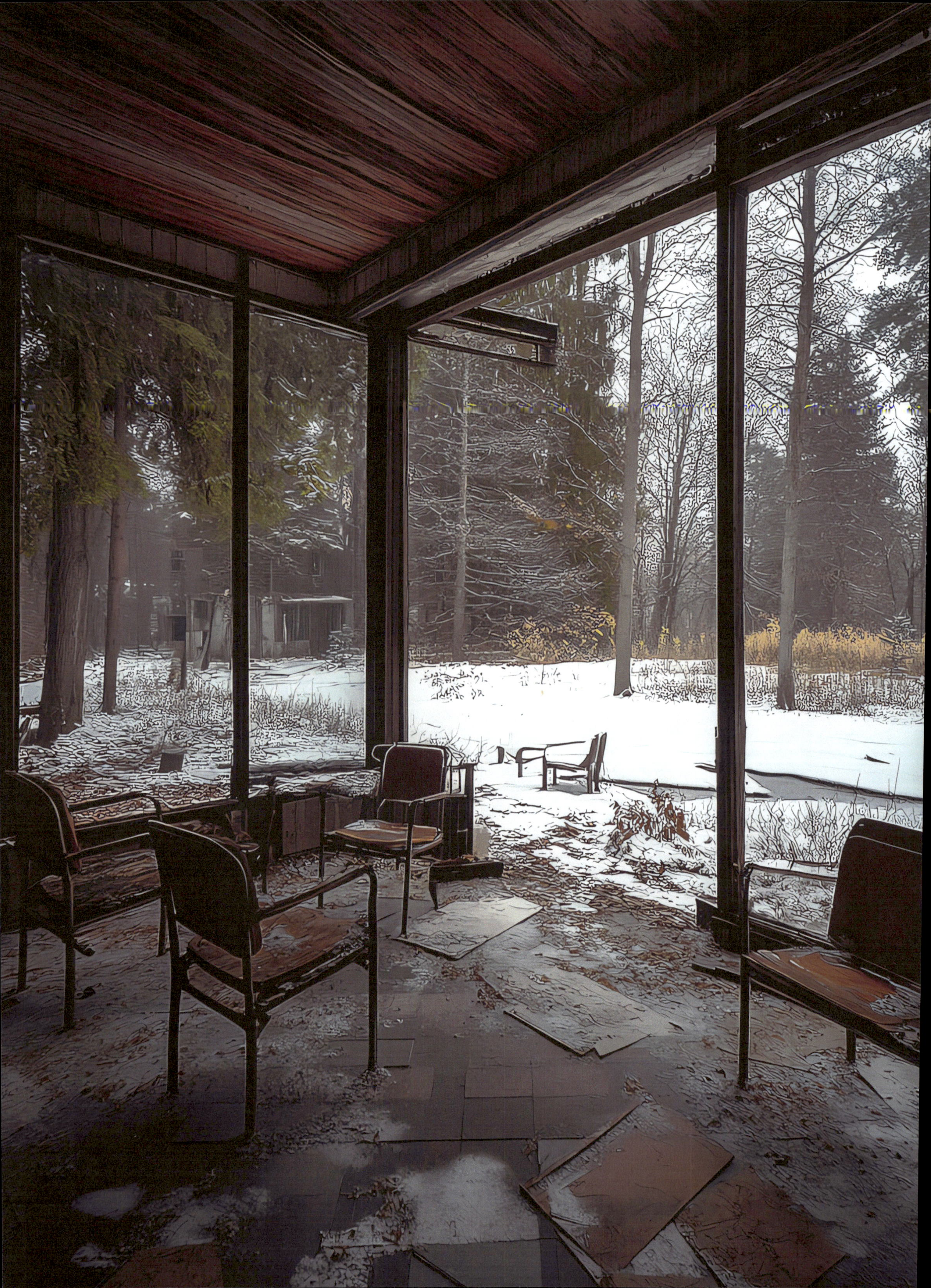

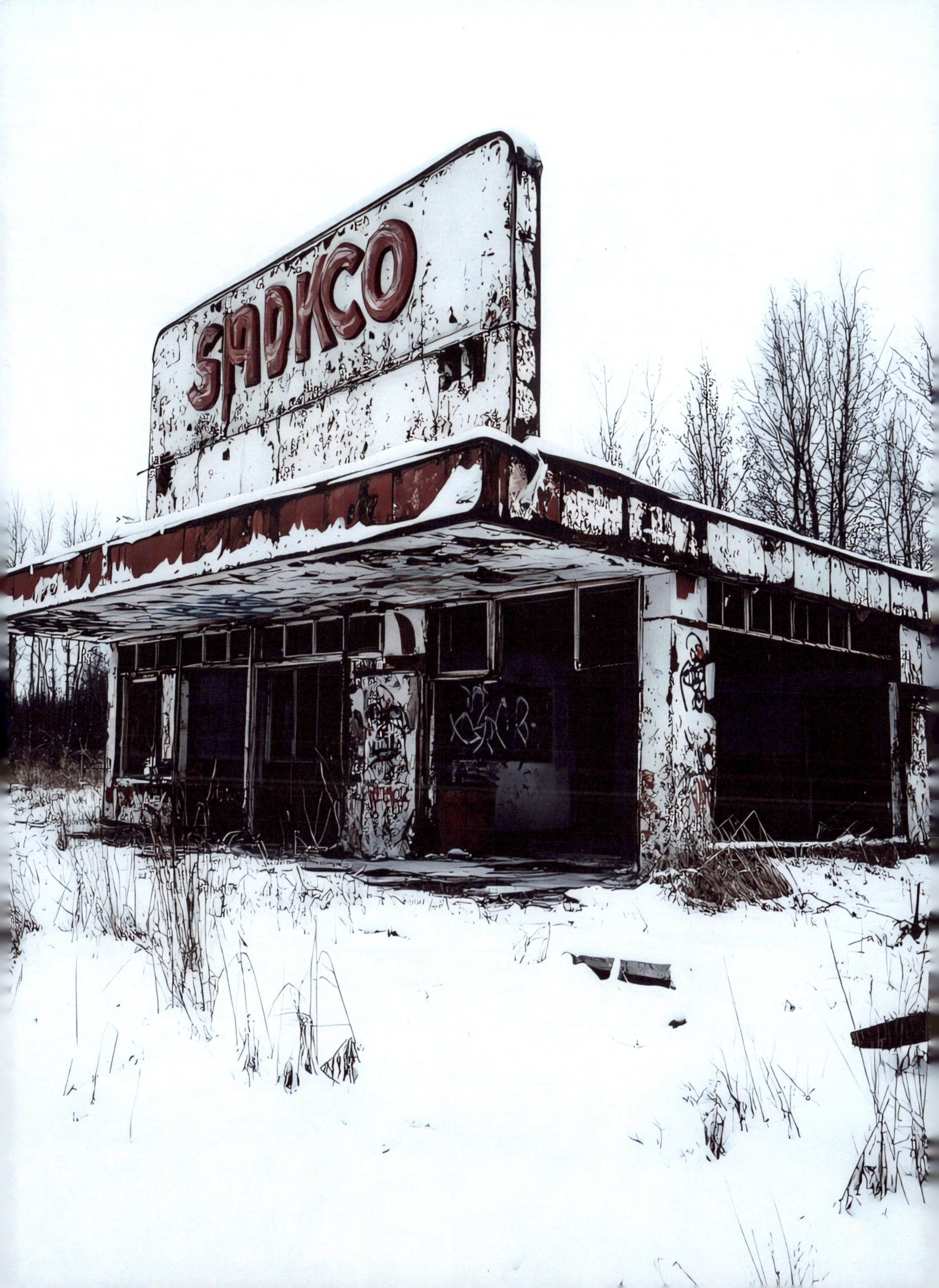
SADKO

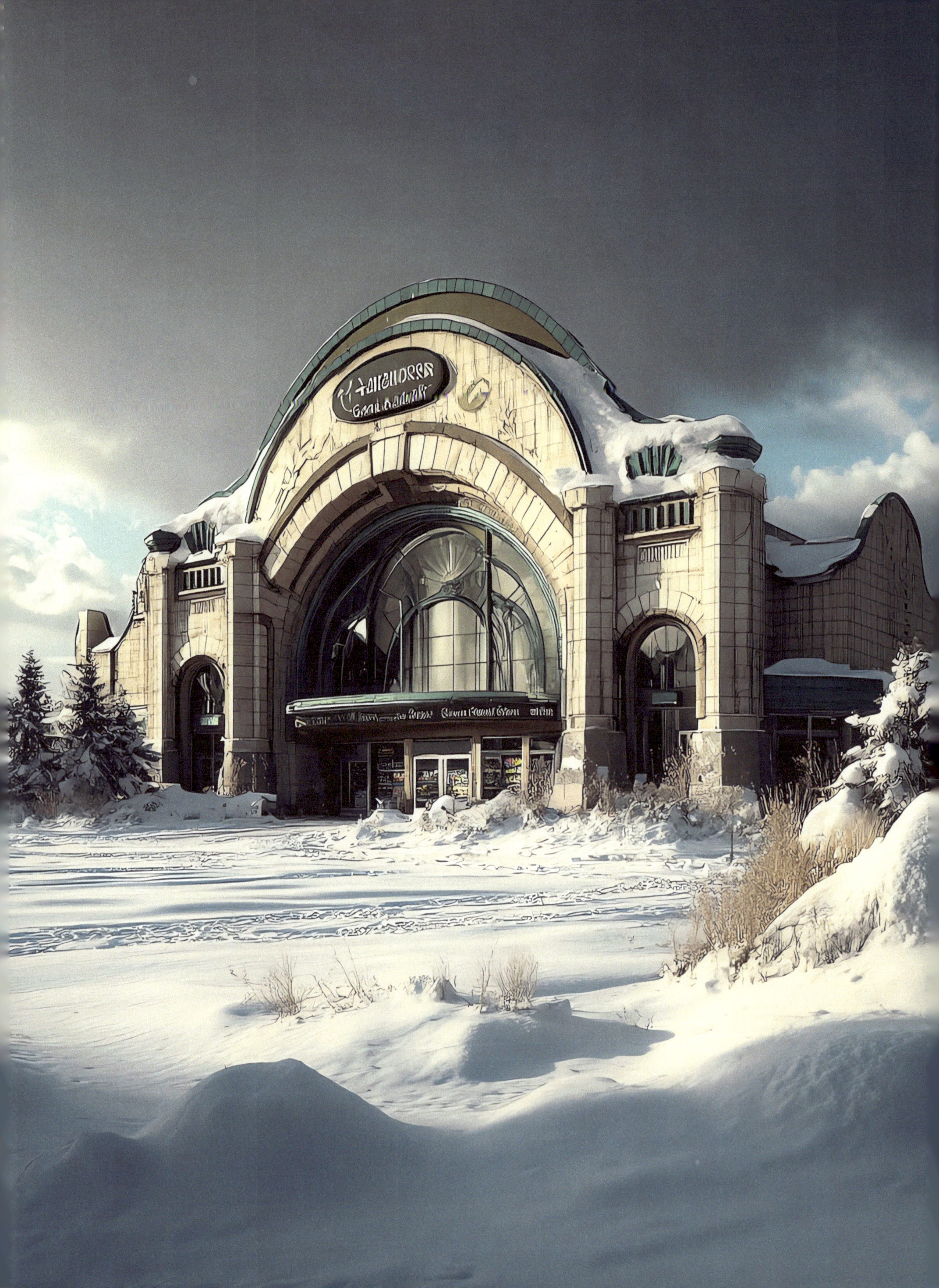

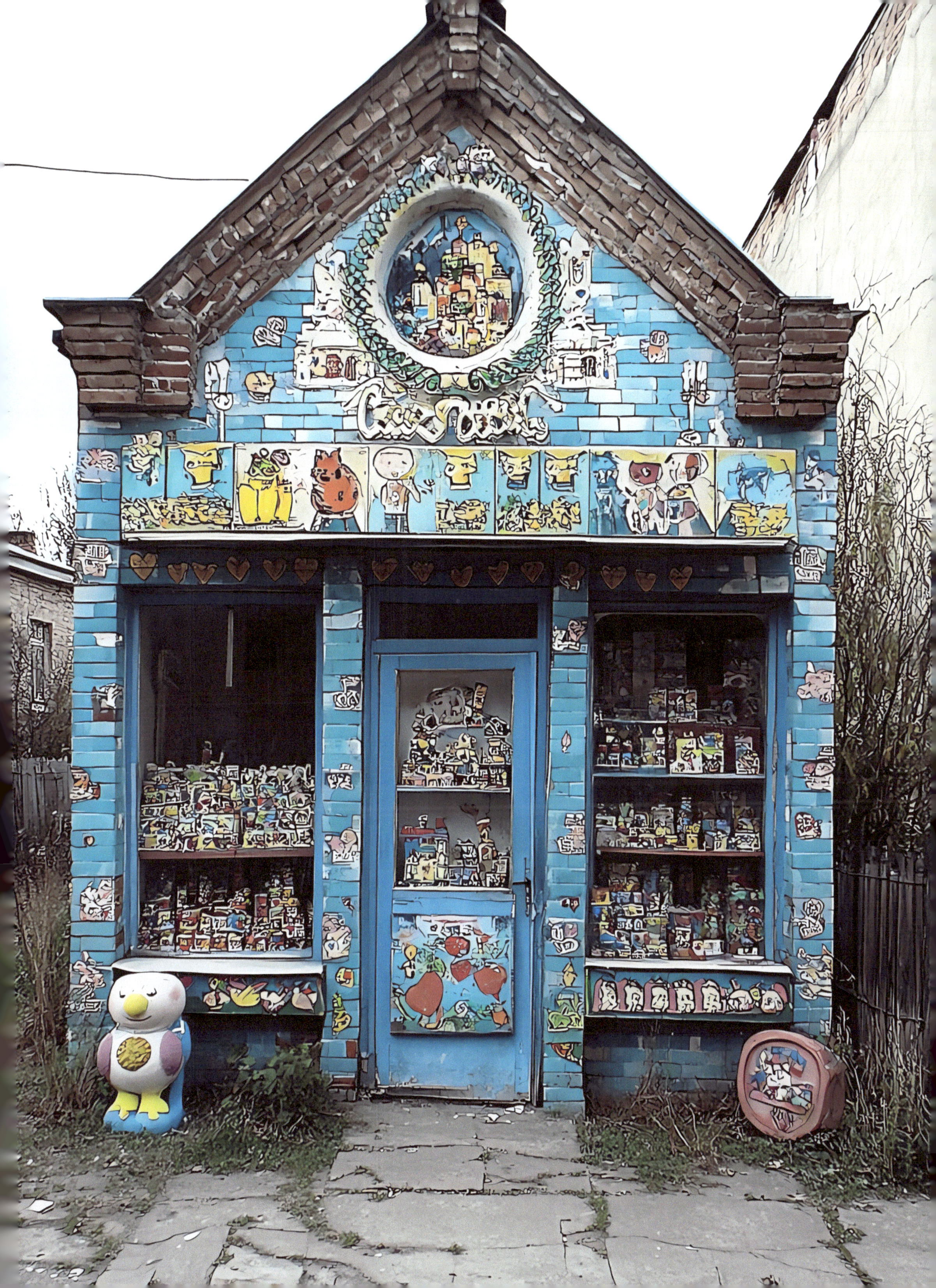

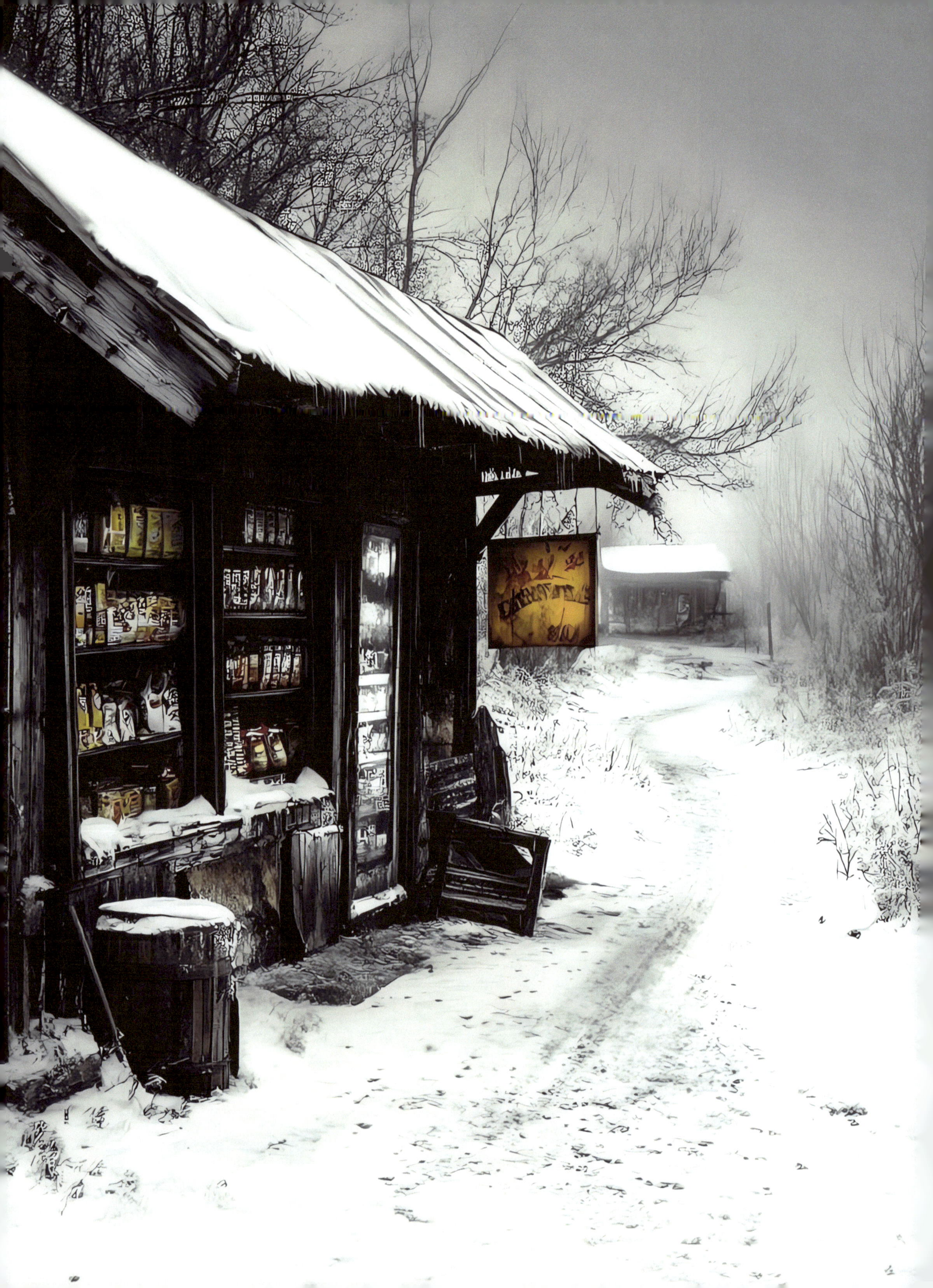

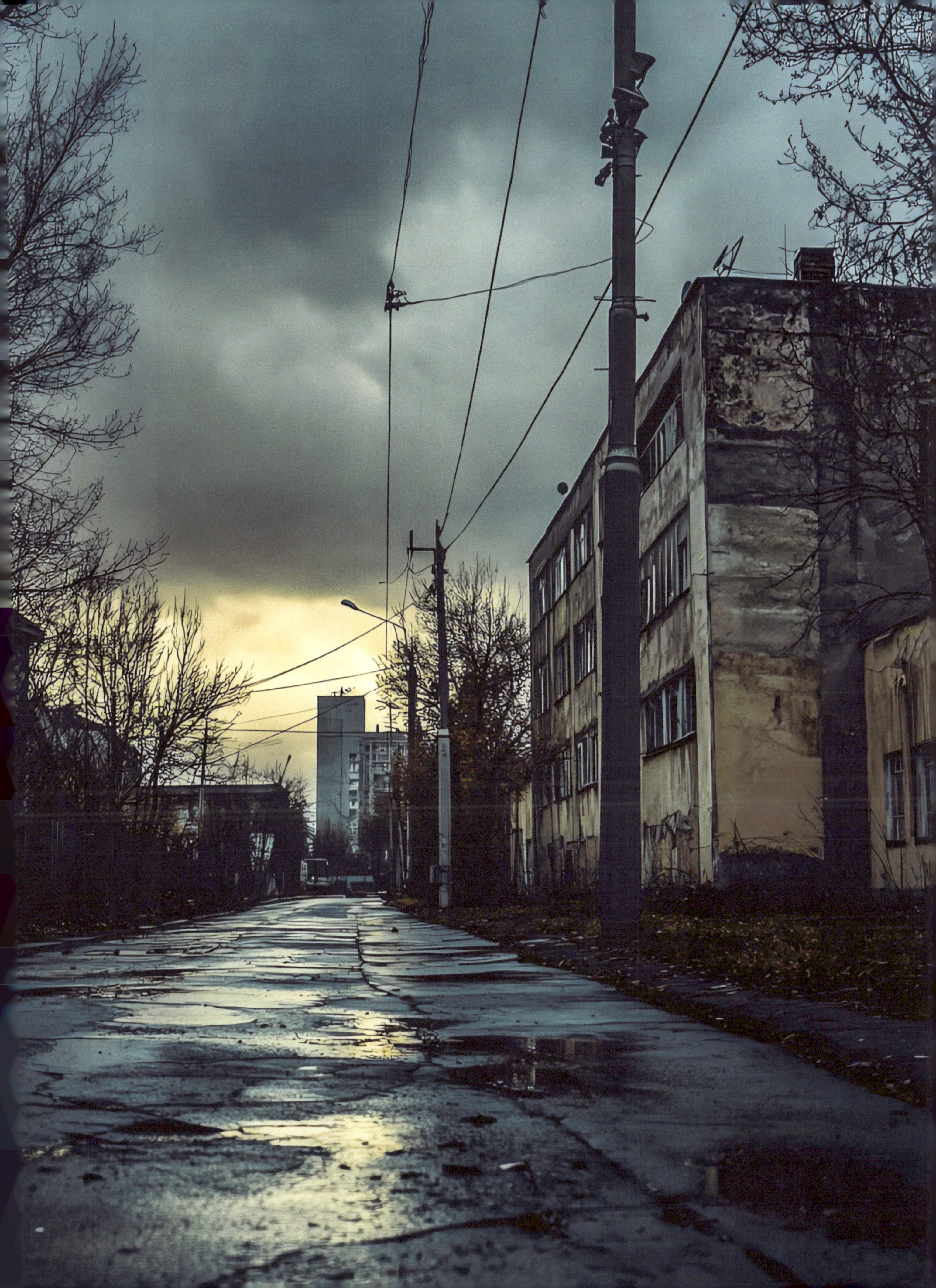

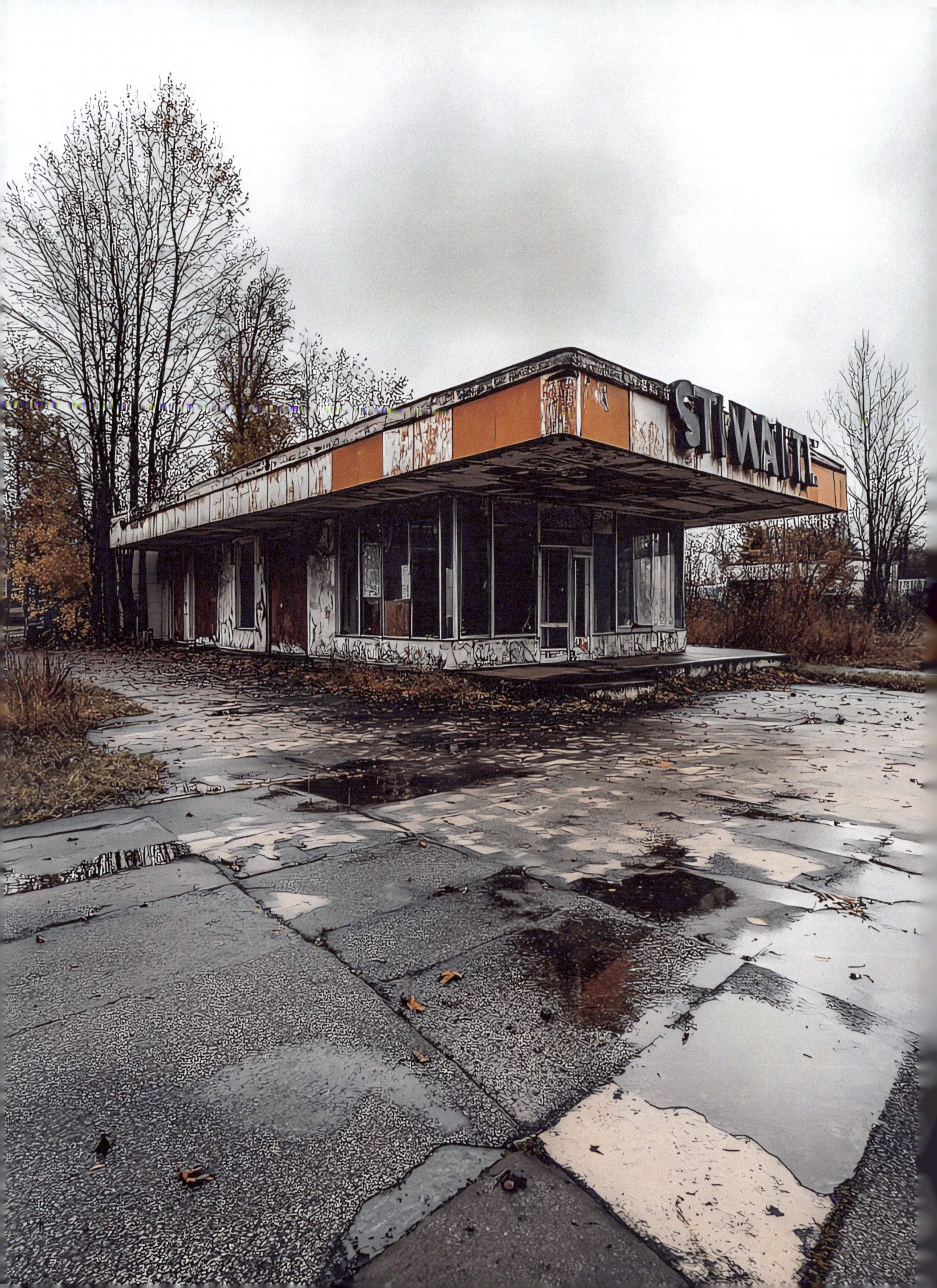

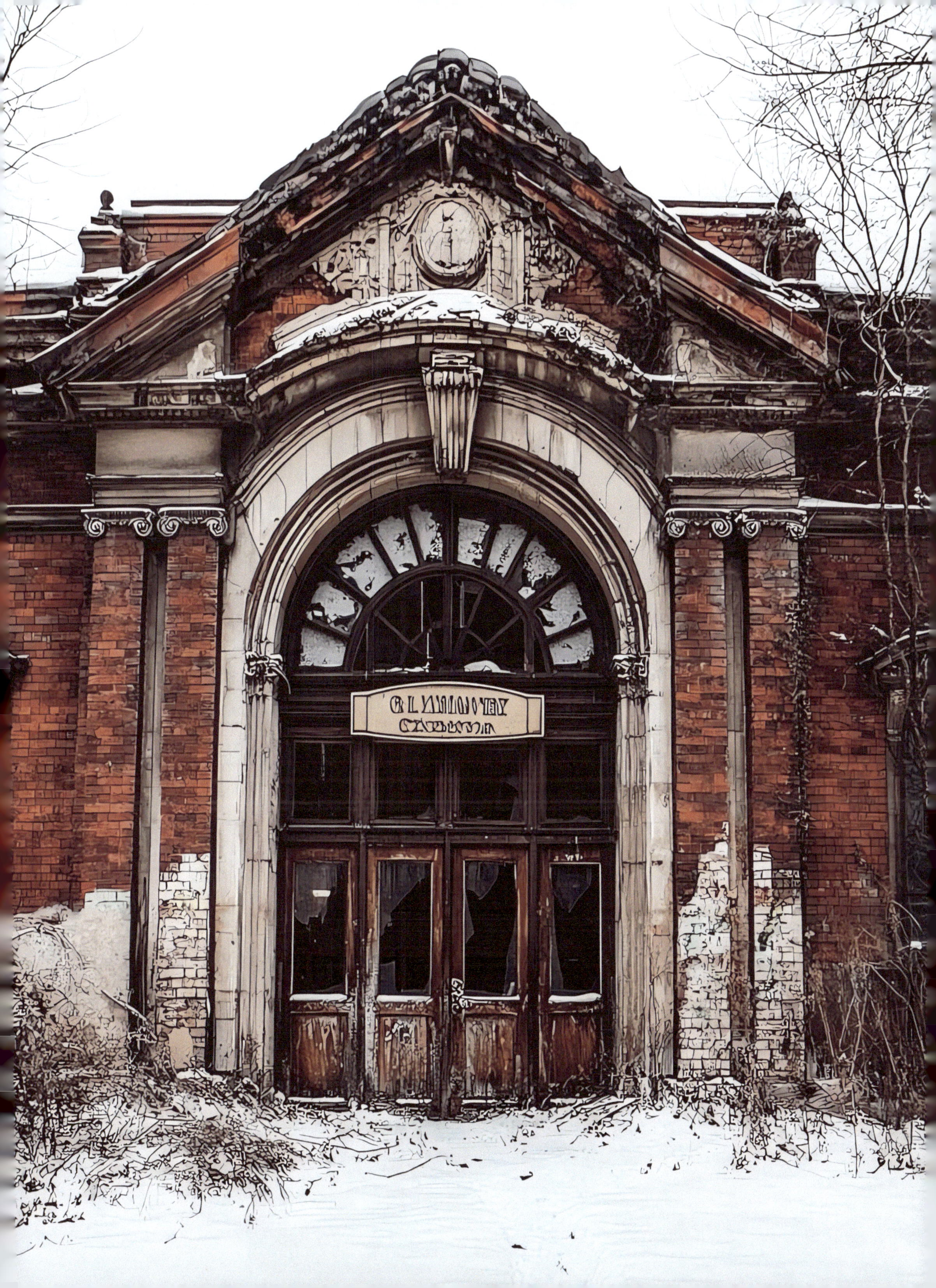

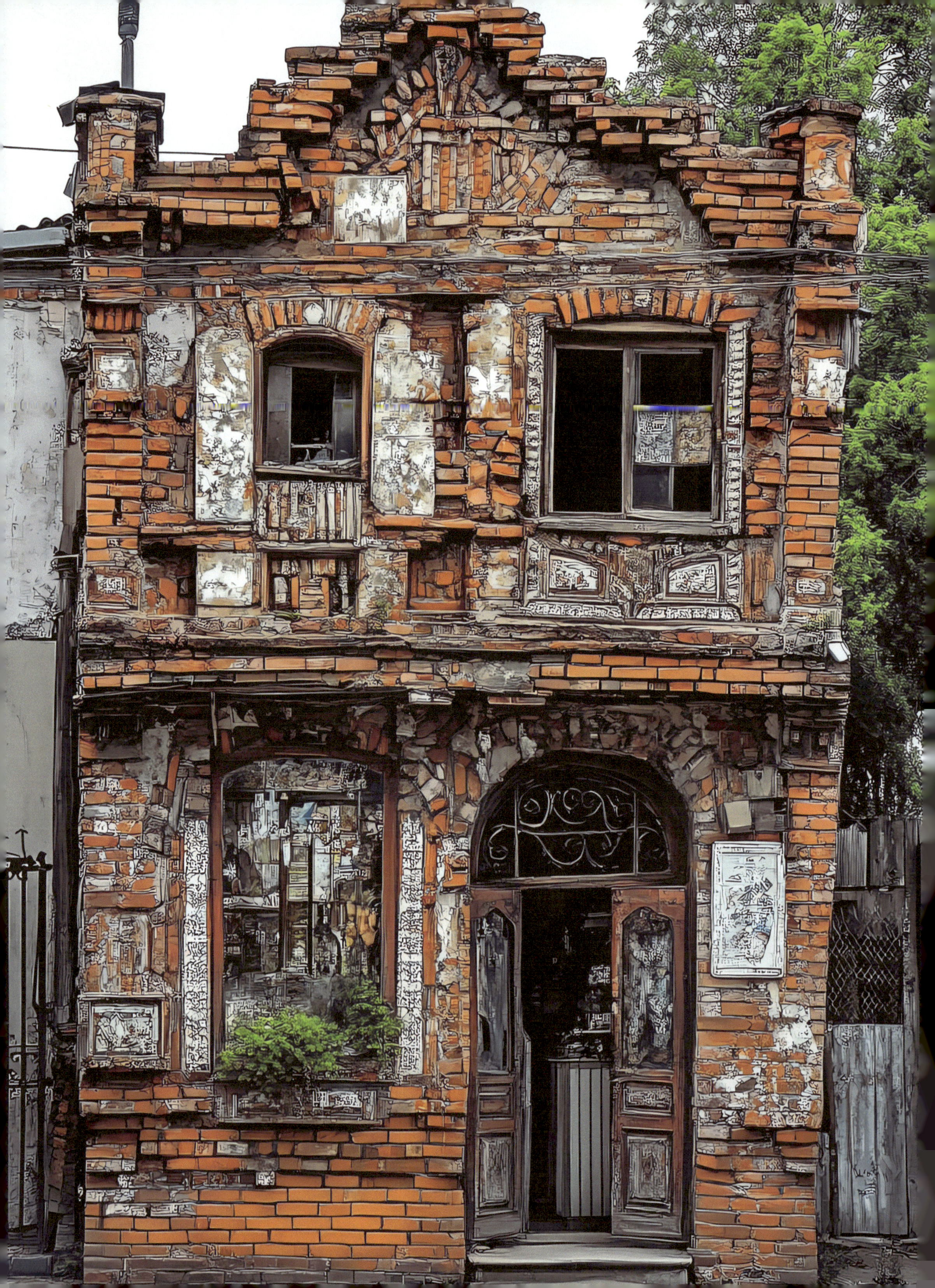

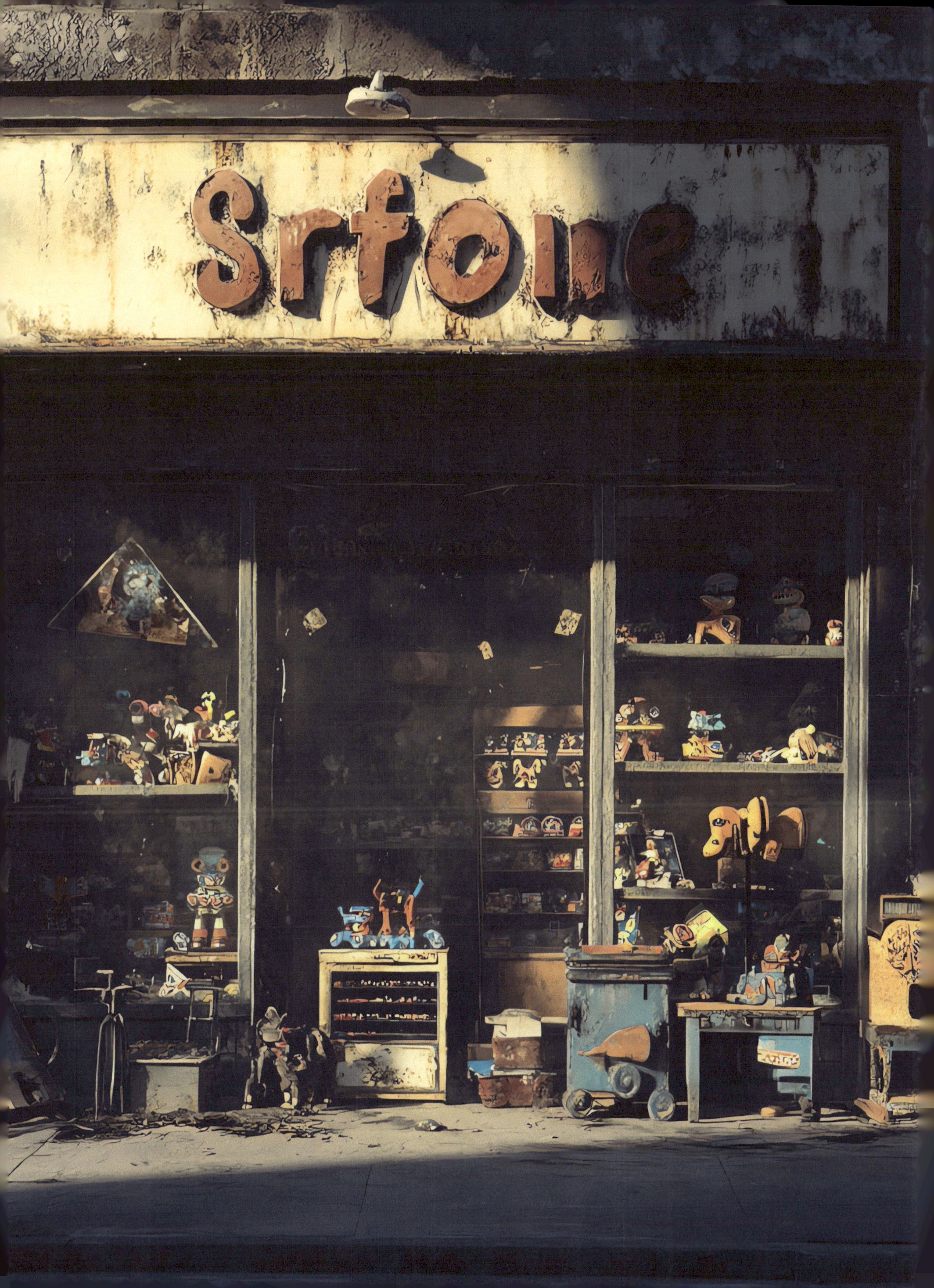

Srfone

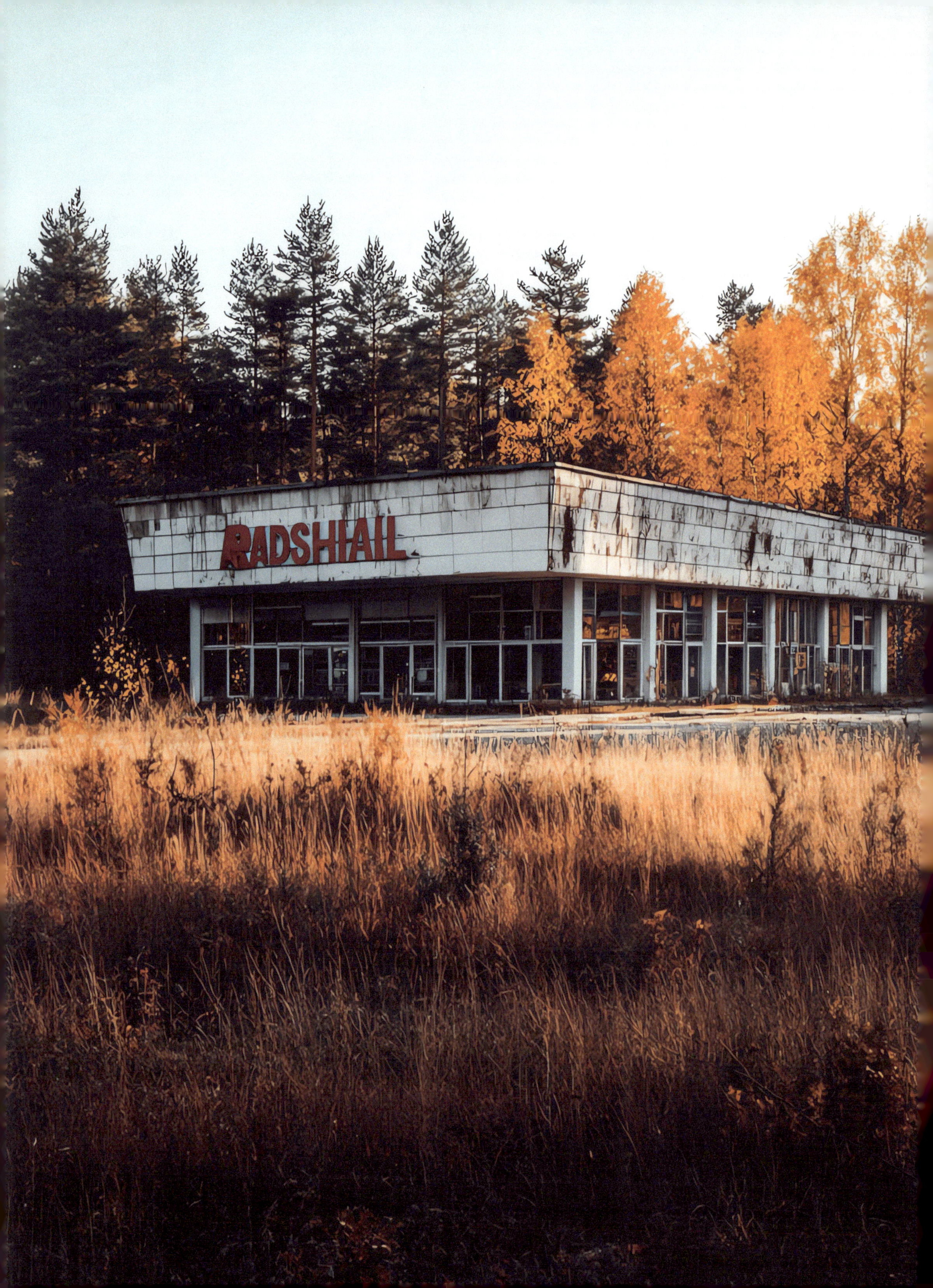

RADSHIAIL

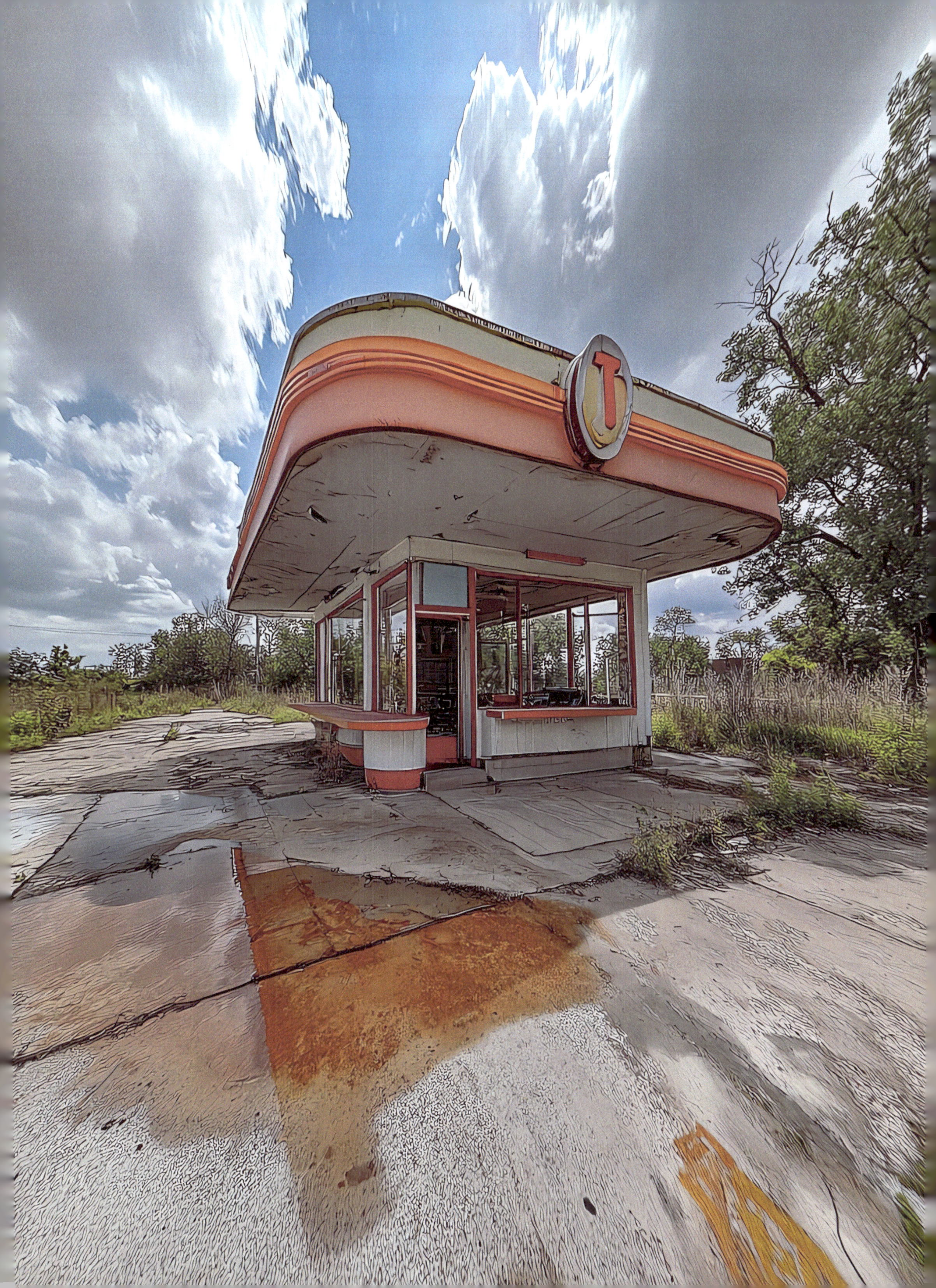

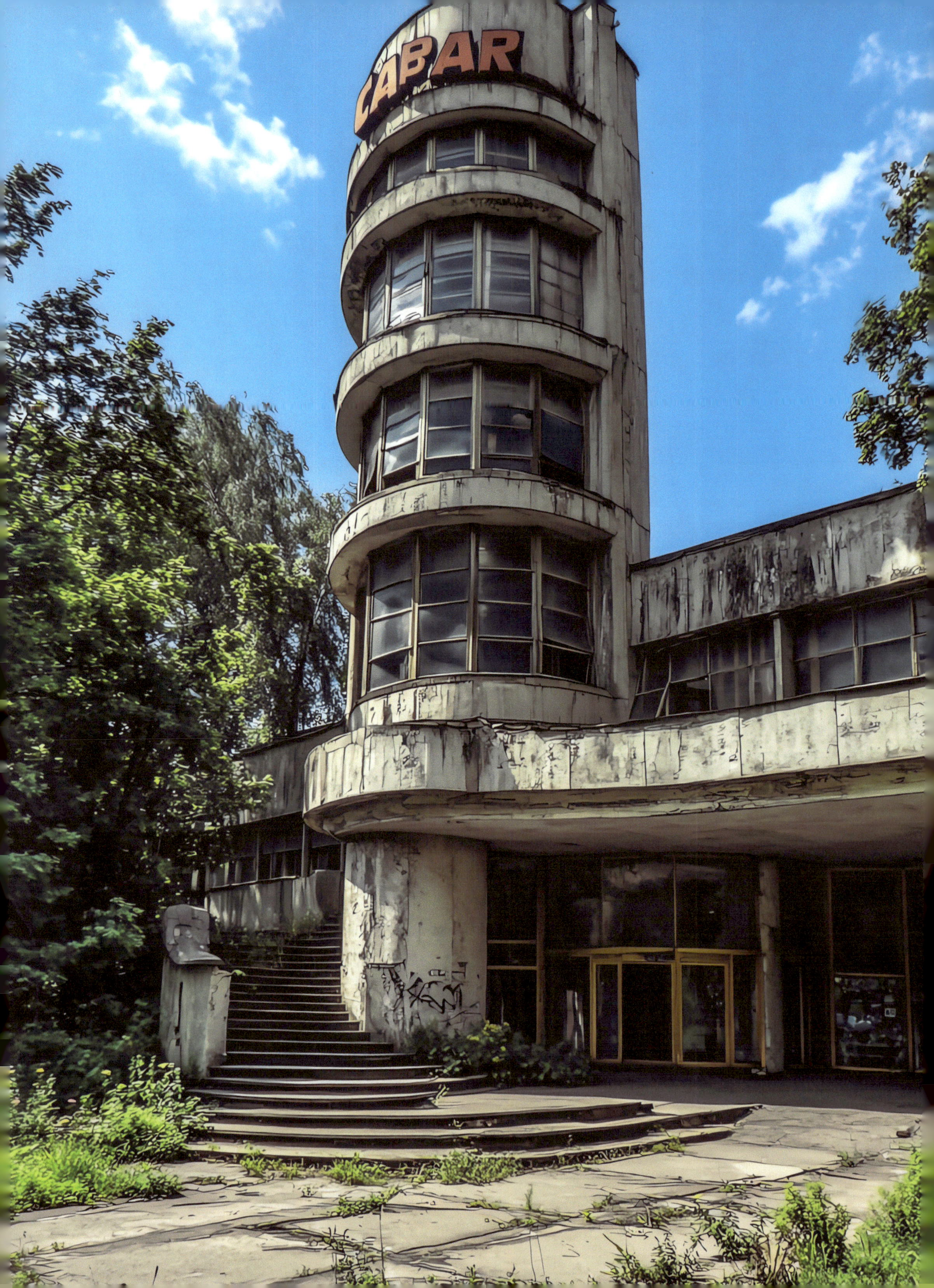
CABAR

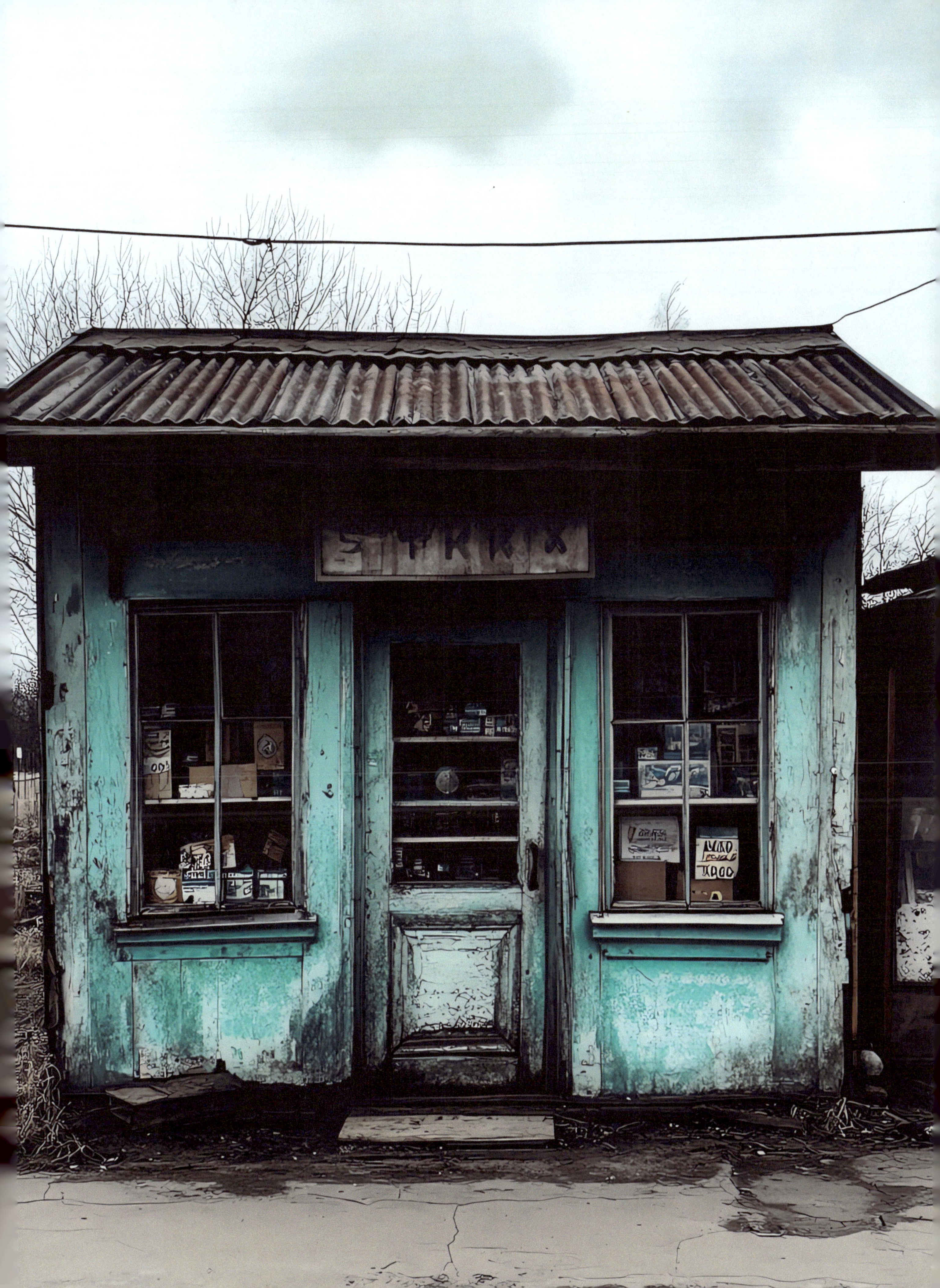

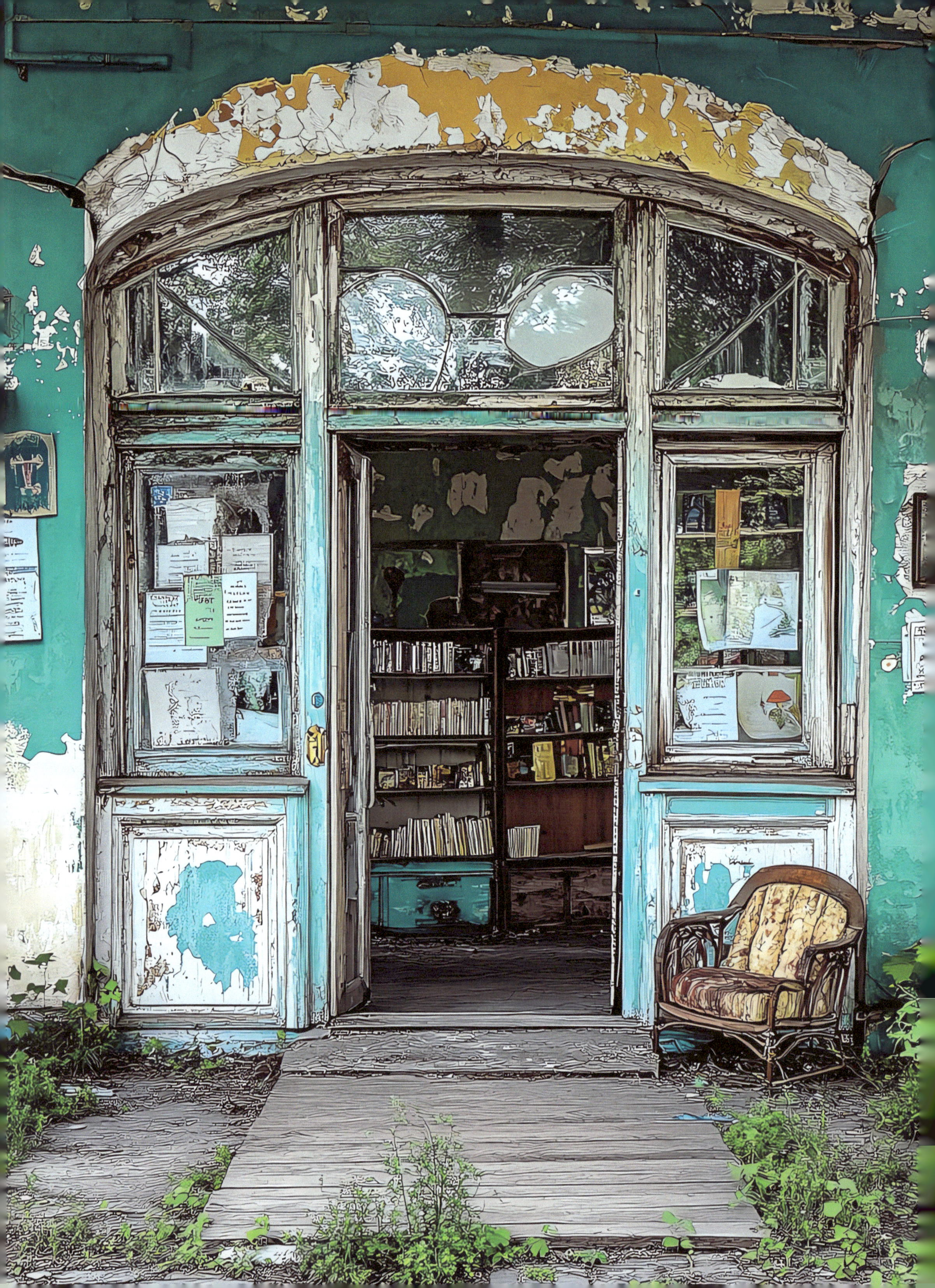

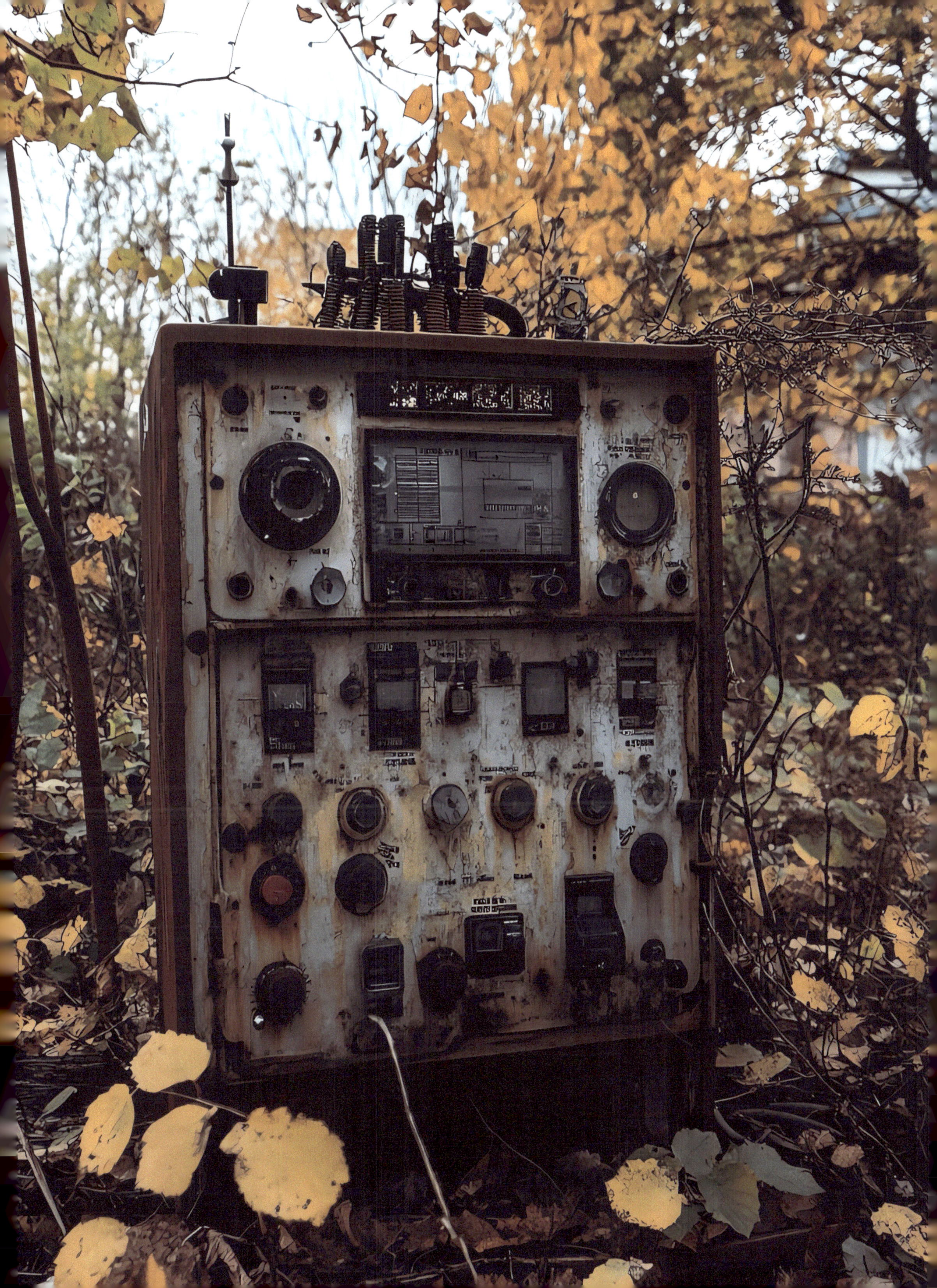

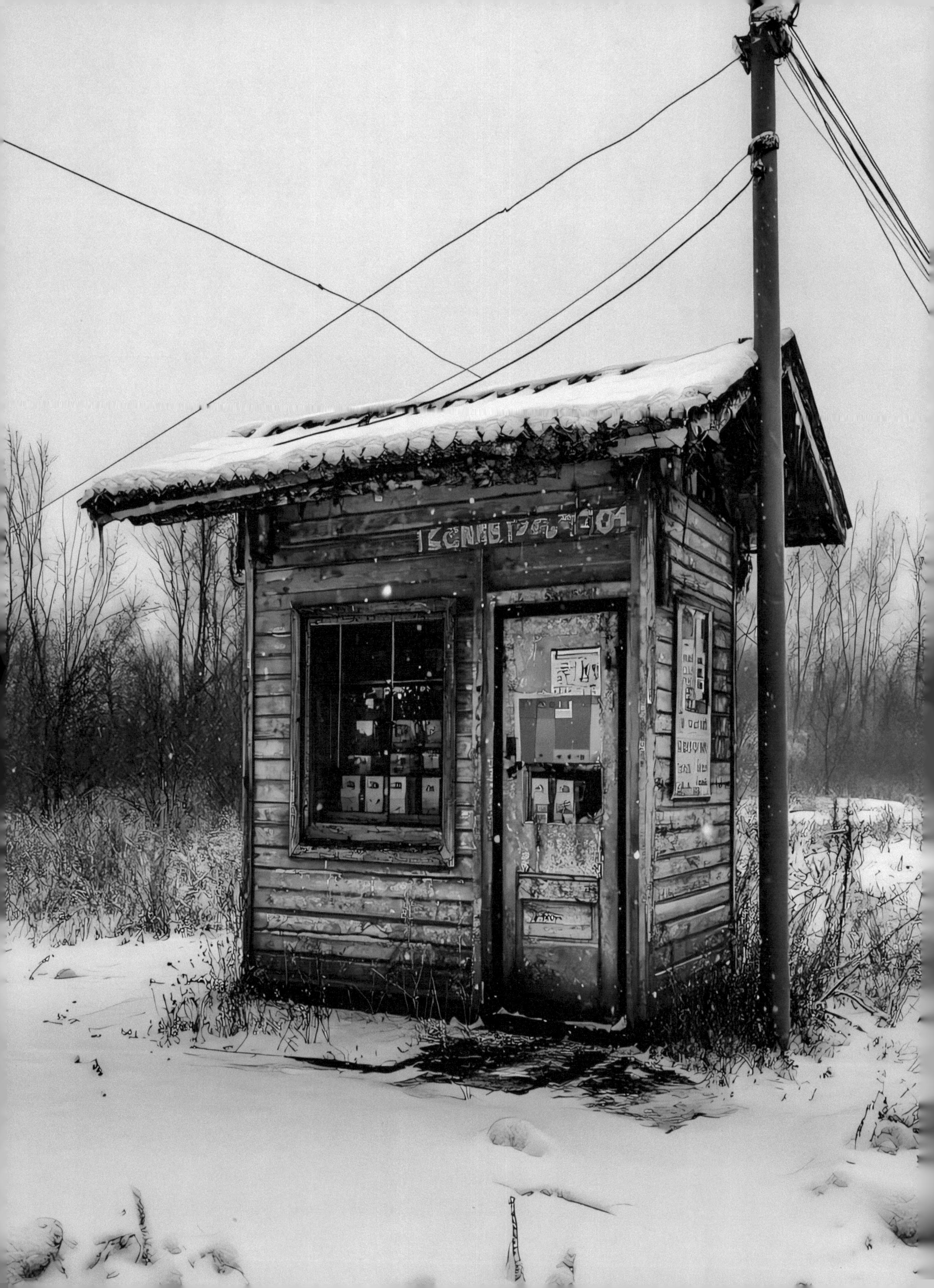

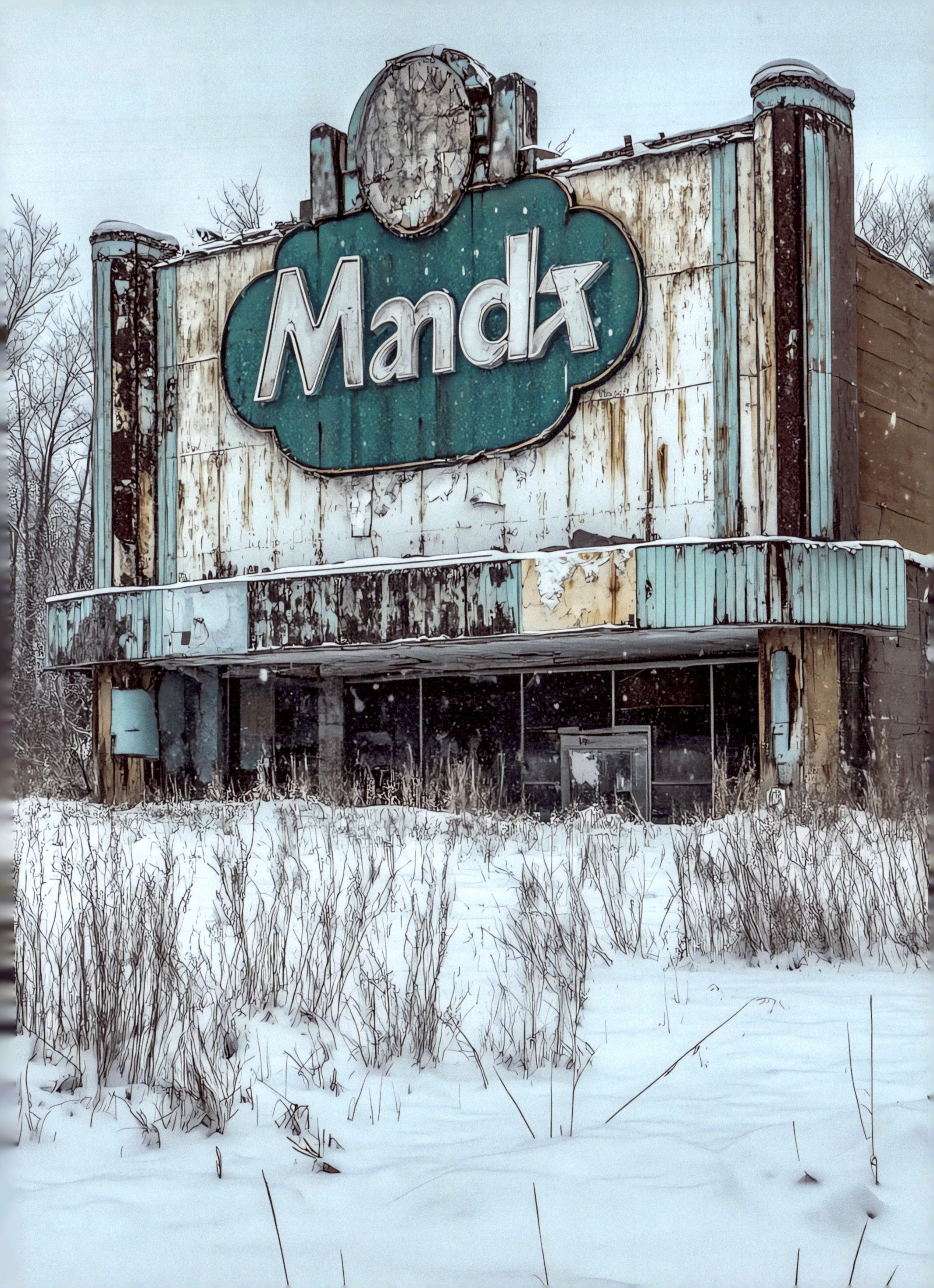
Mandx

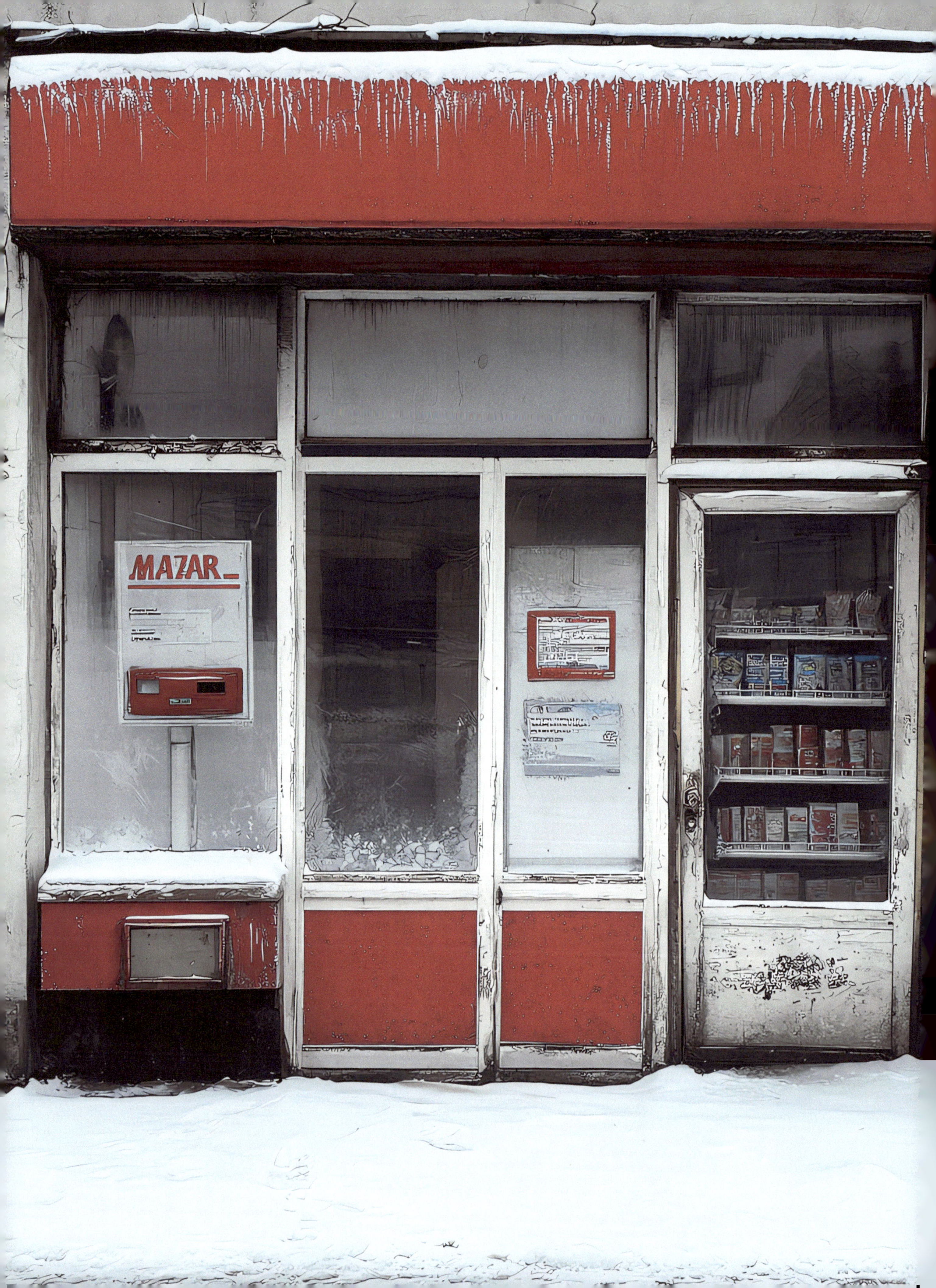
MAZAR

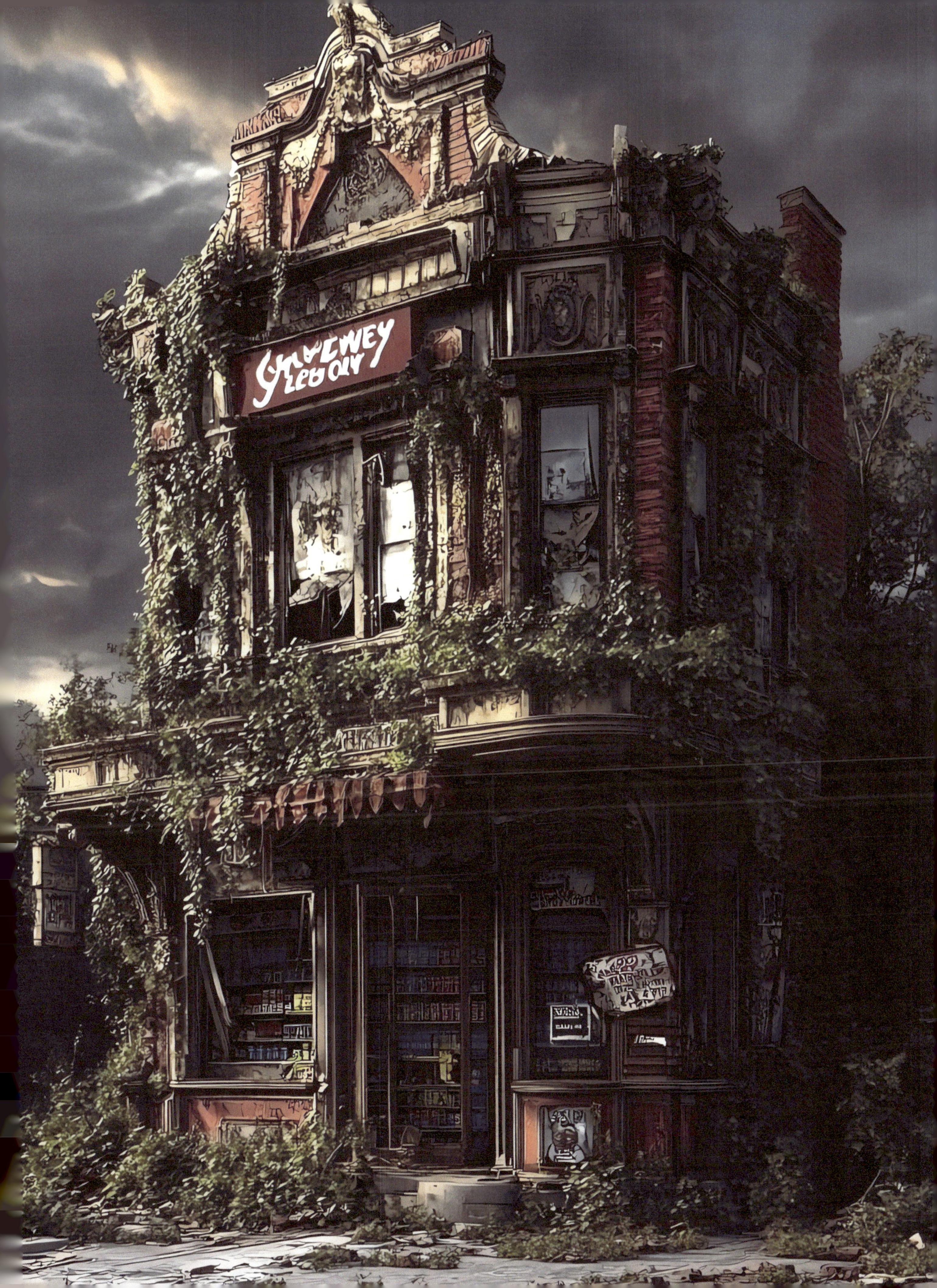

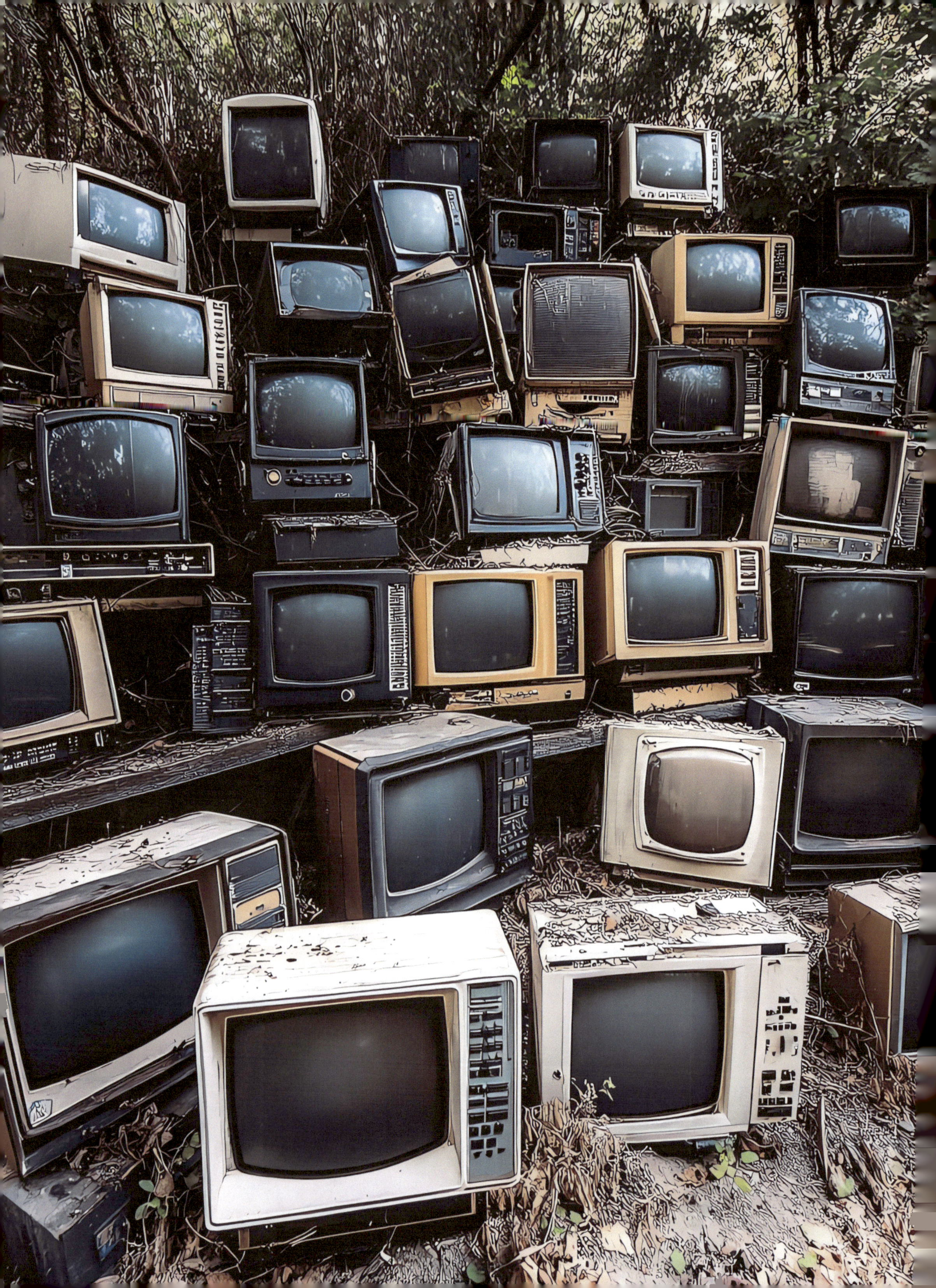

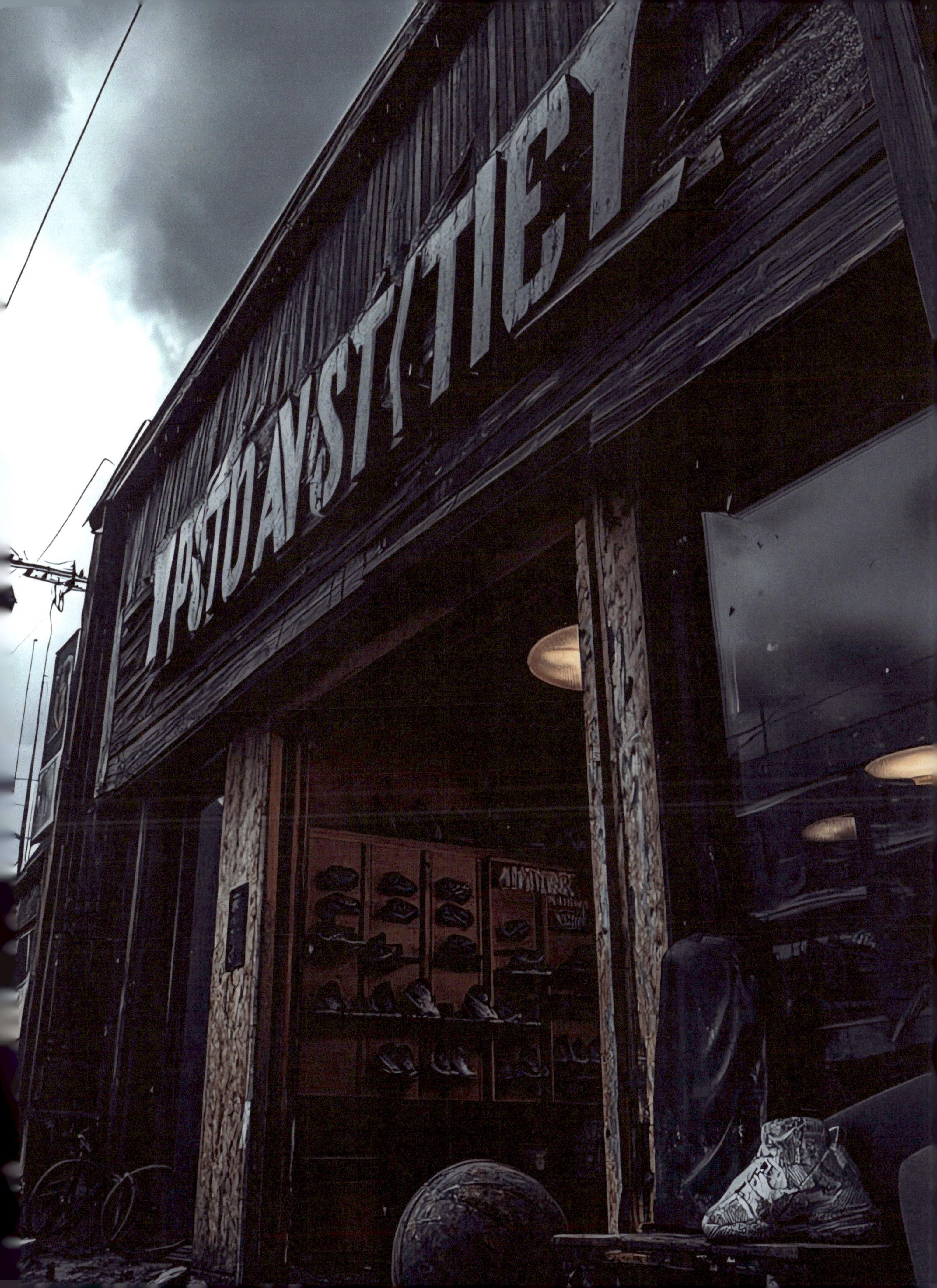
YPSTUAVSTTIET

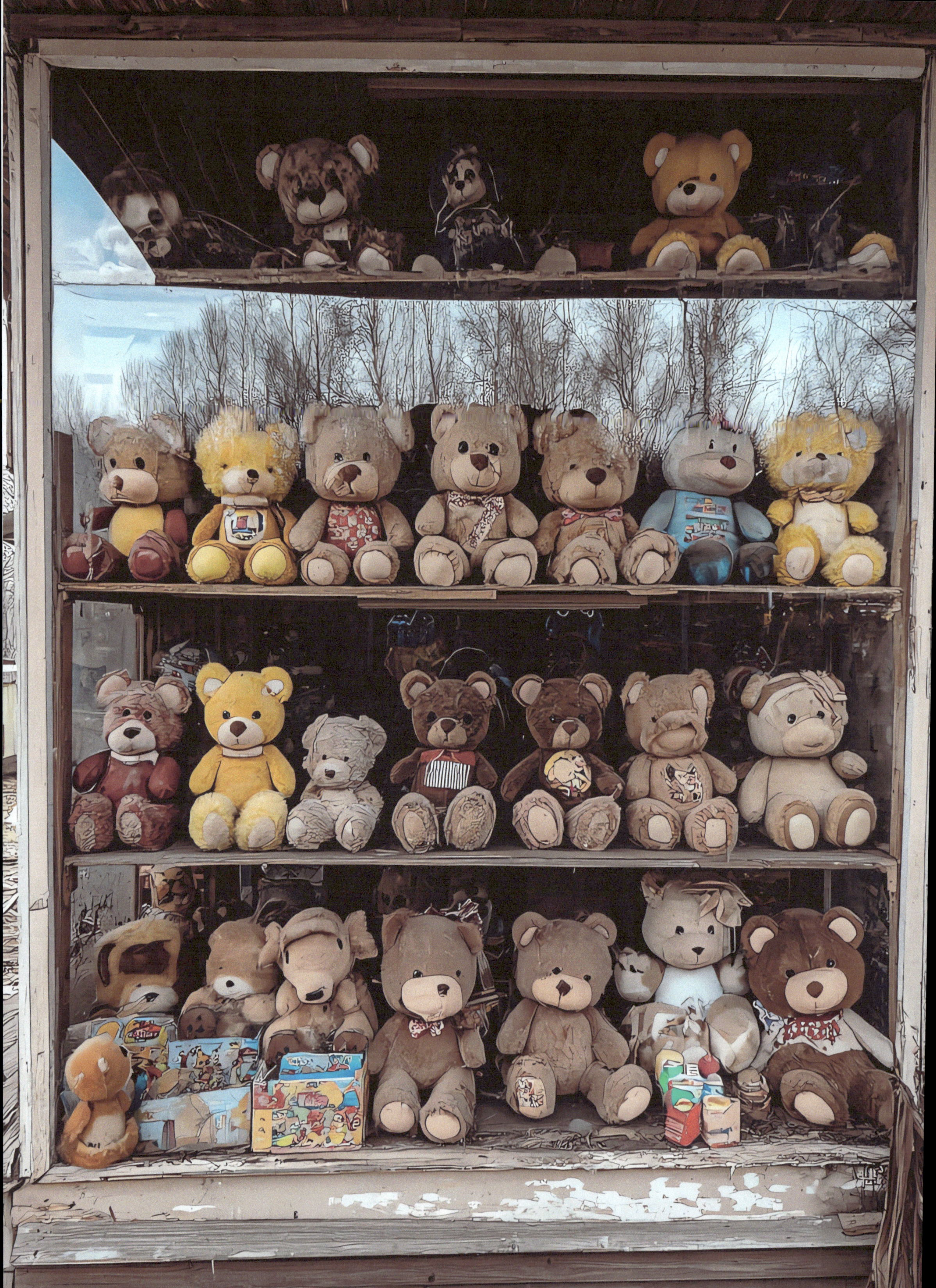

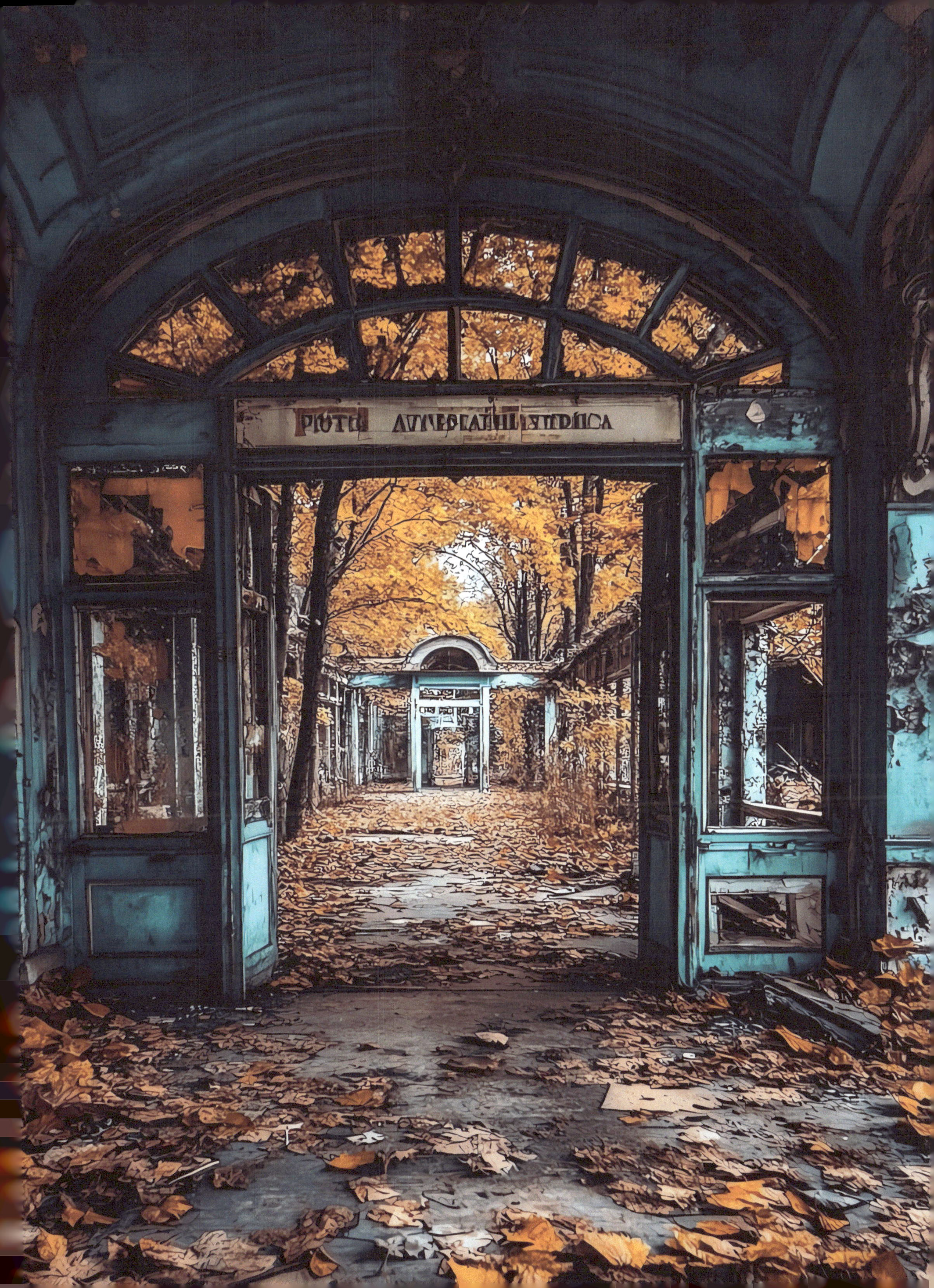

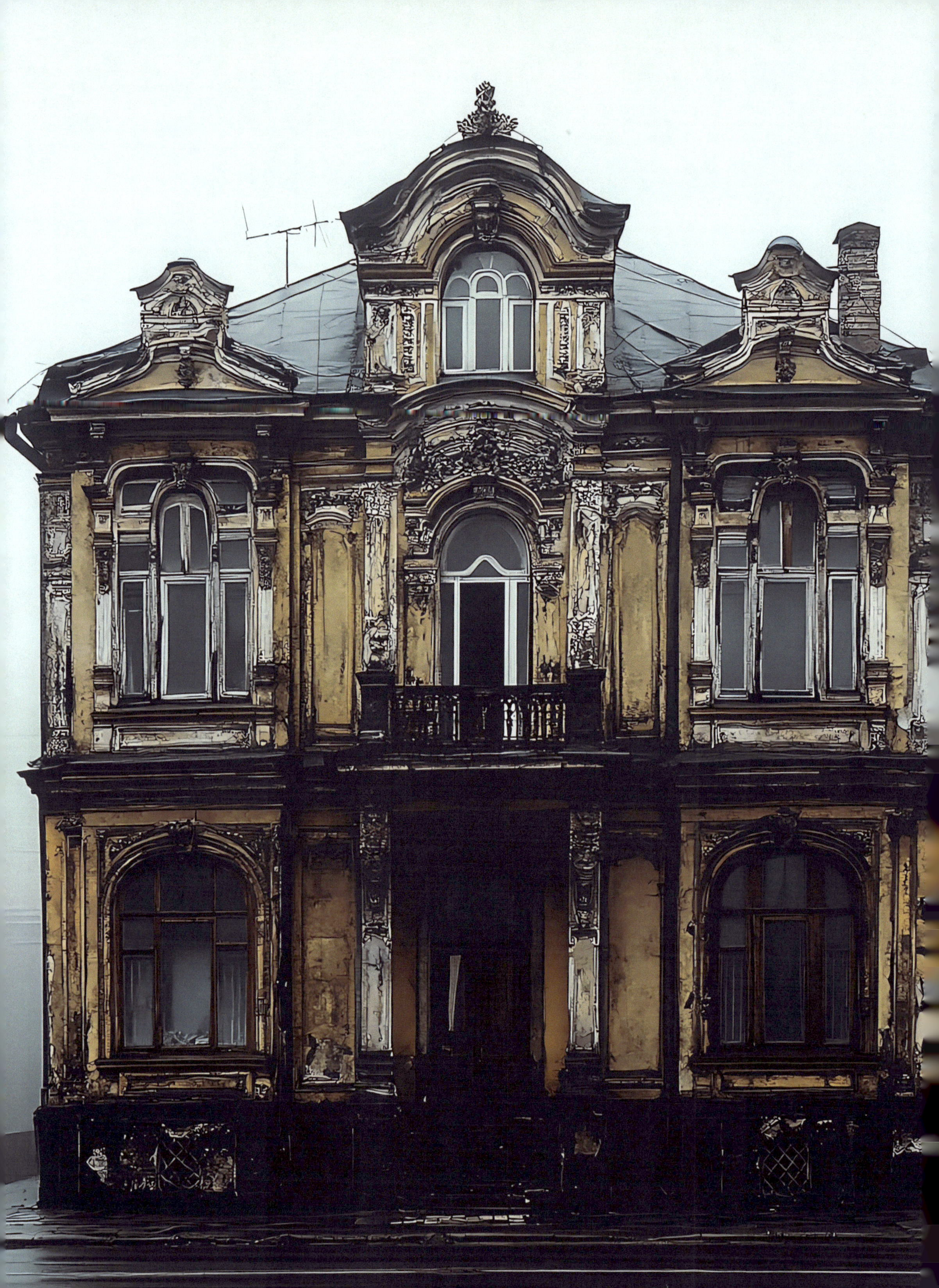

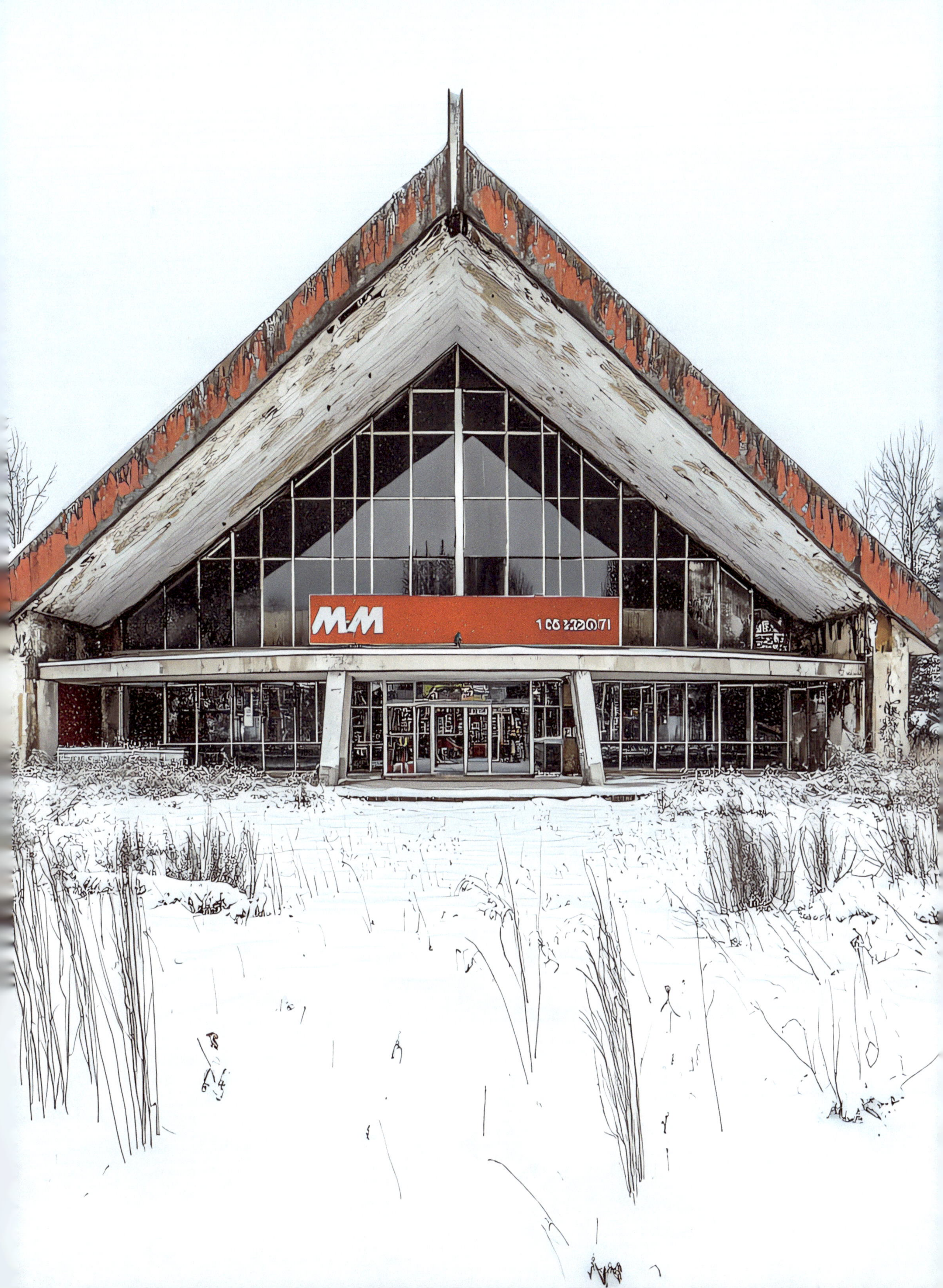
MM

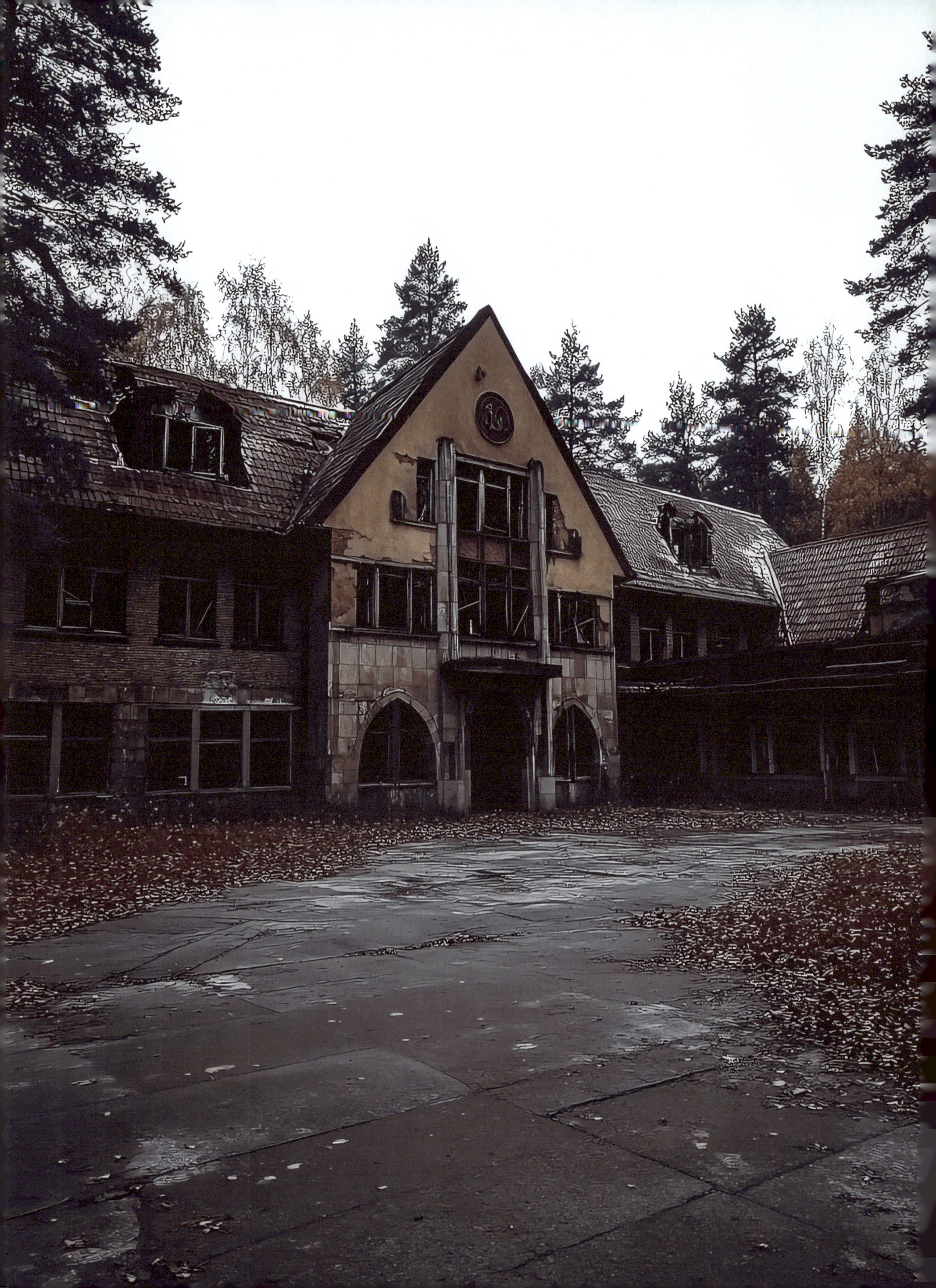

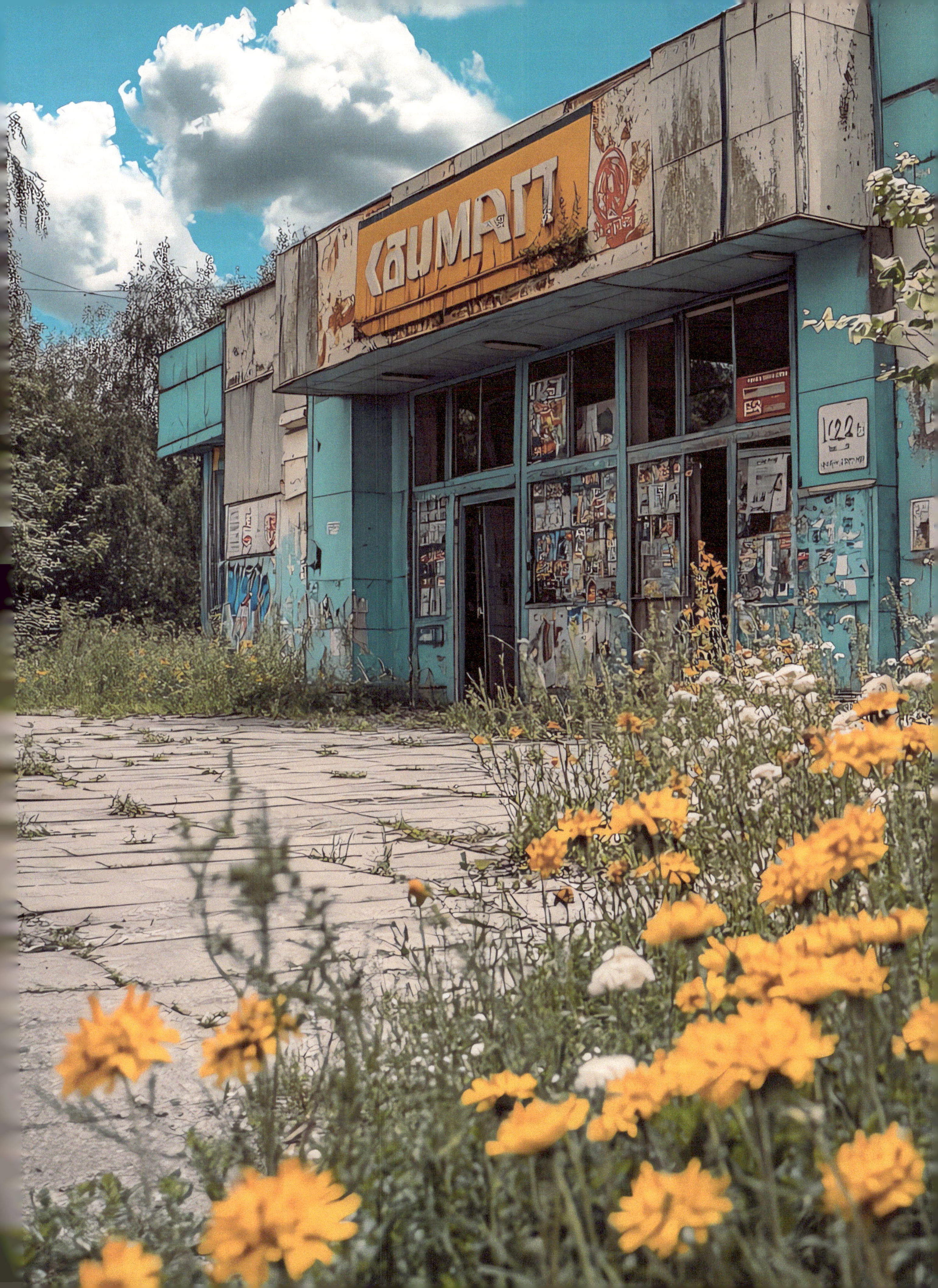
КЛУМАГ

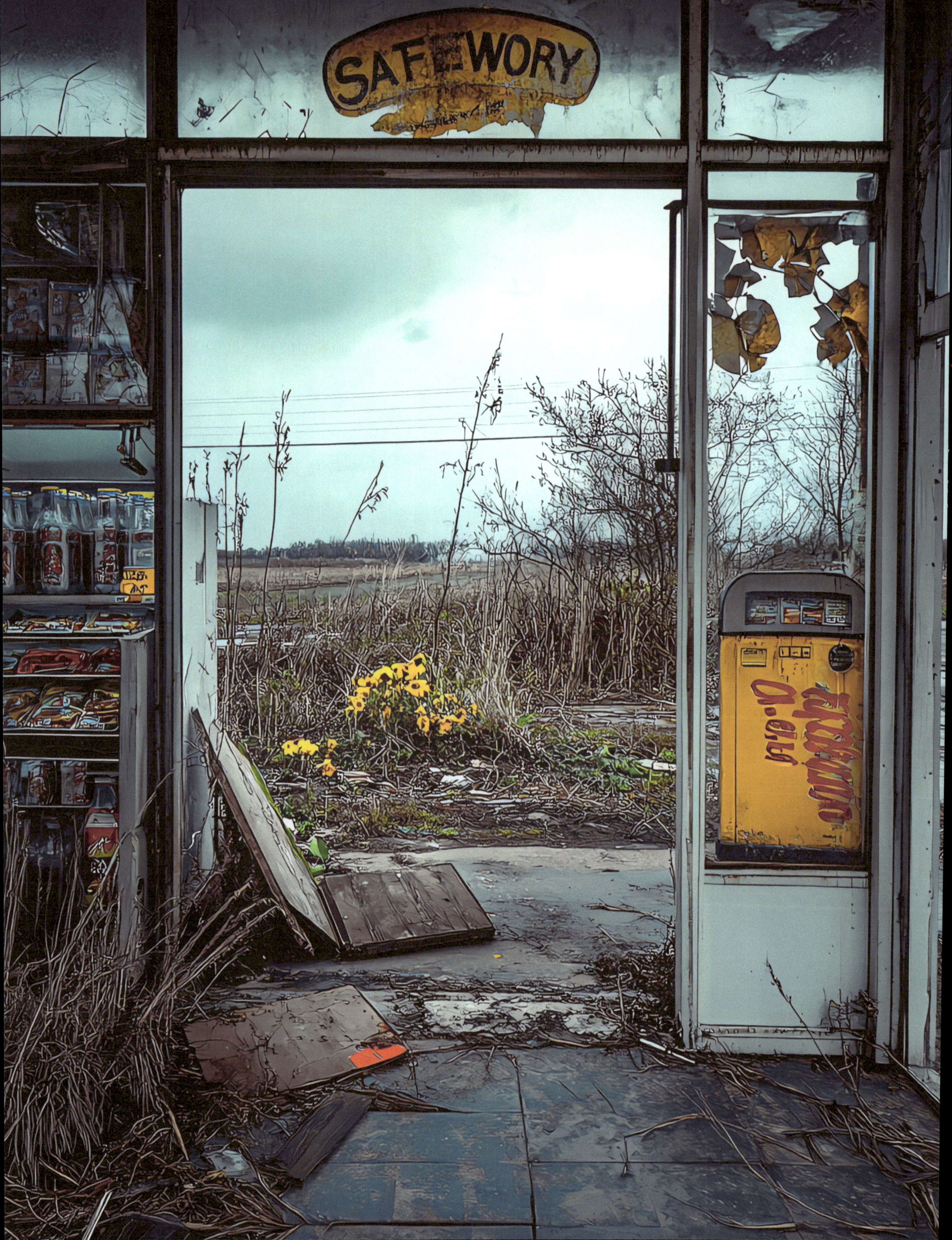

SAFEWORY

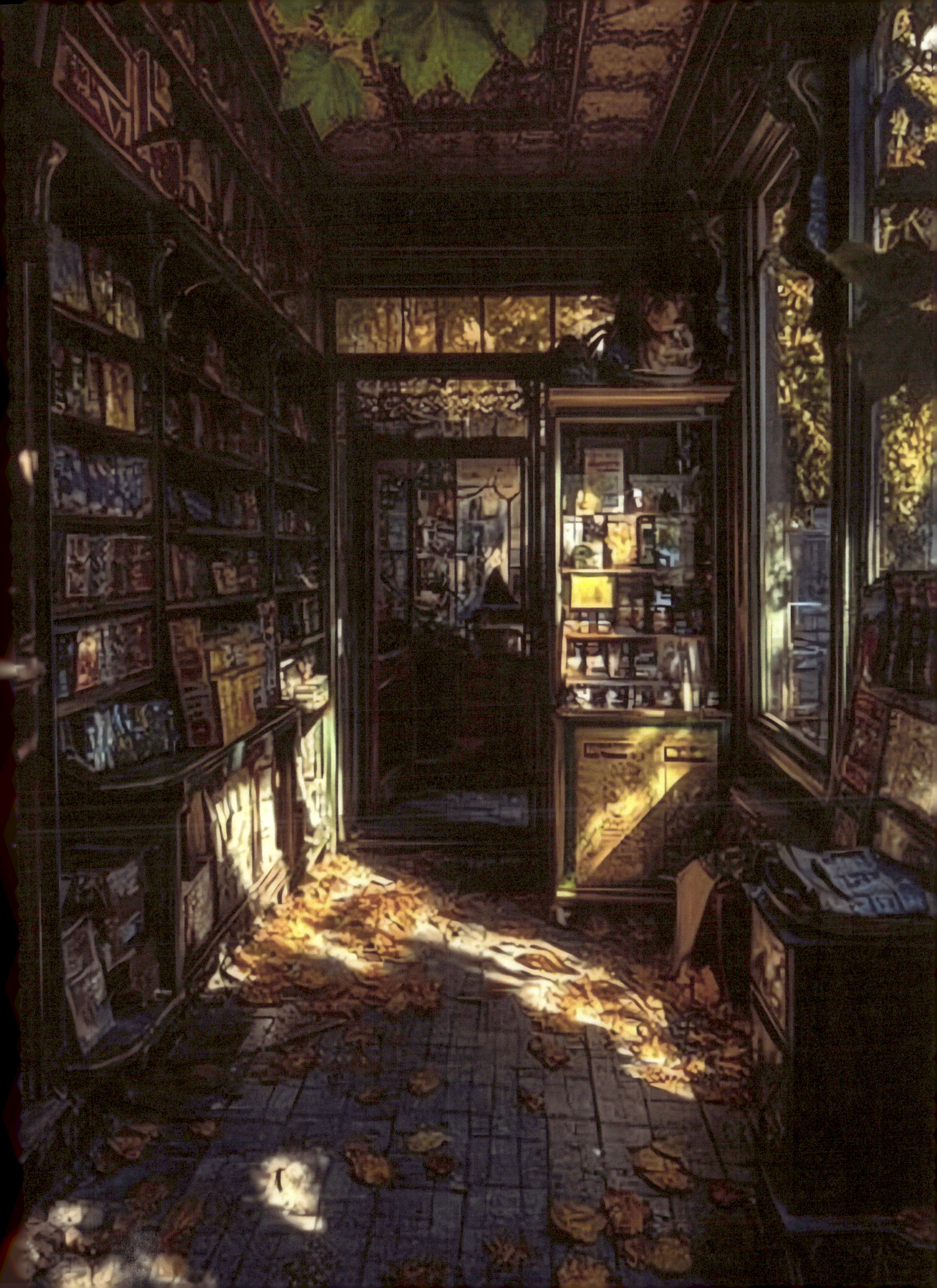

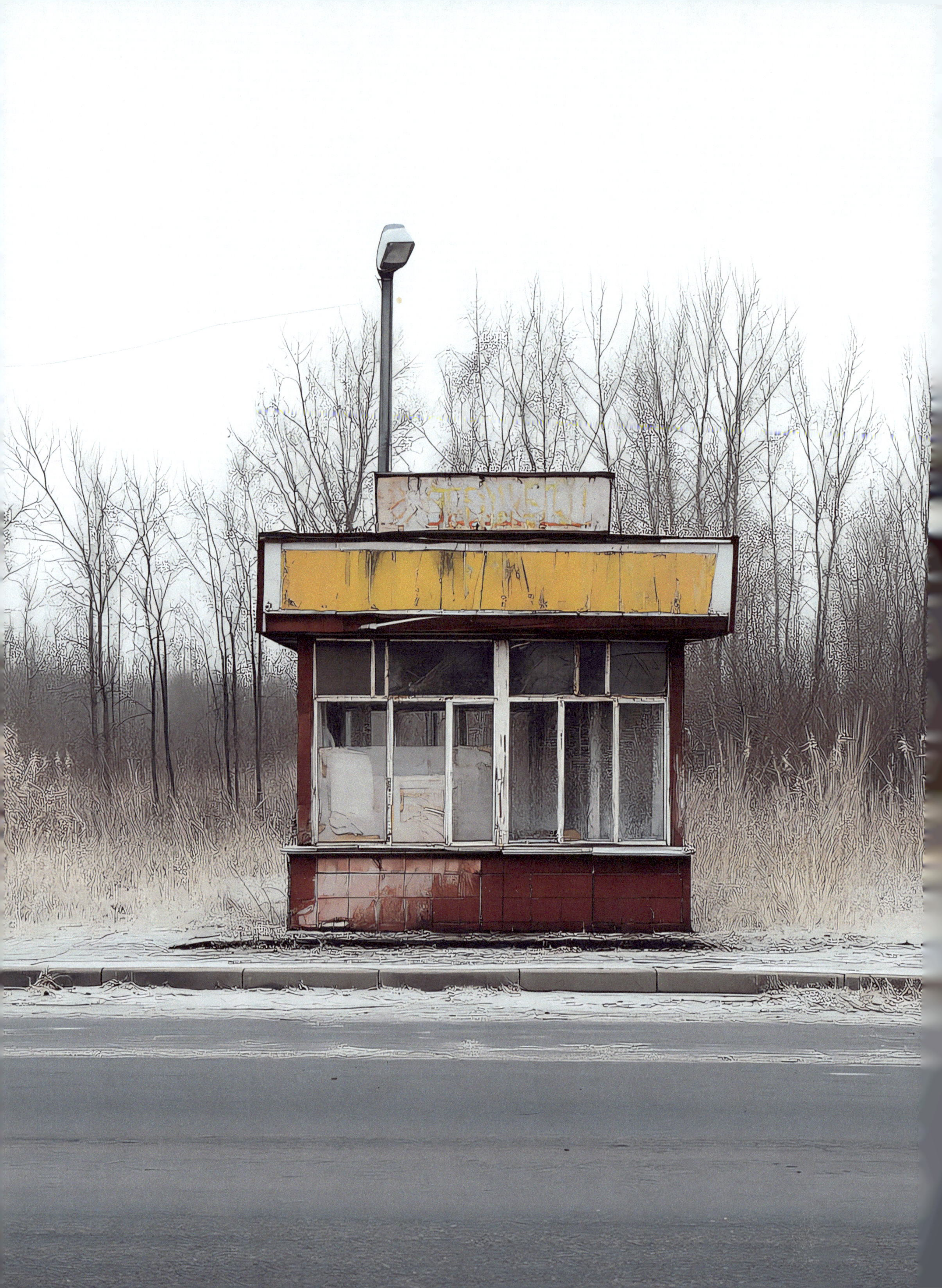

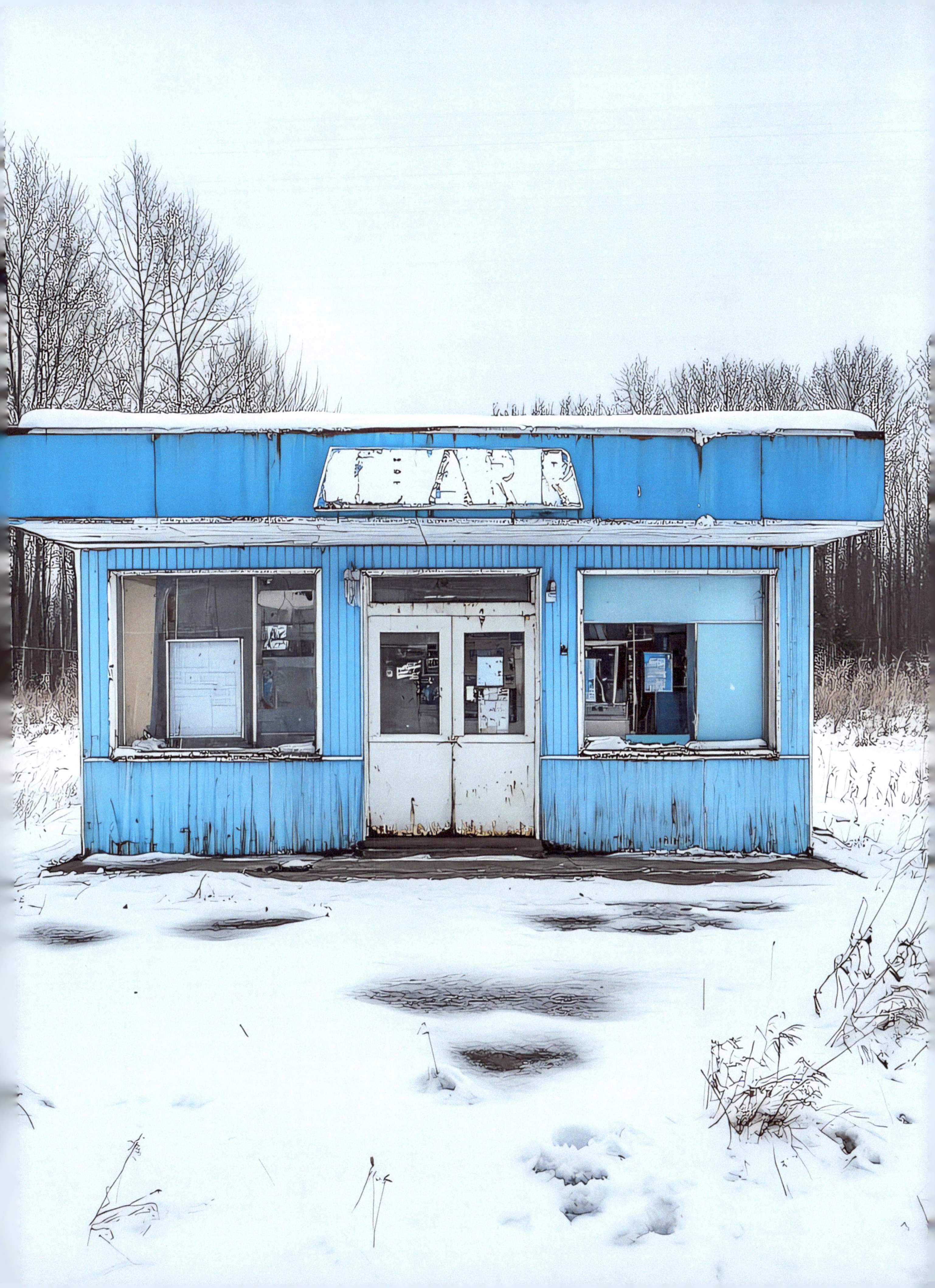
BAR

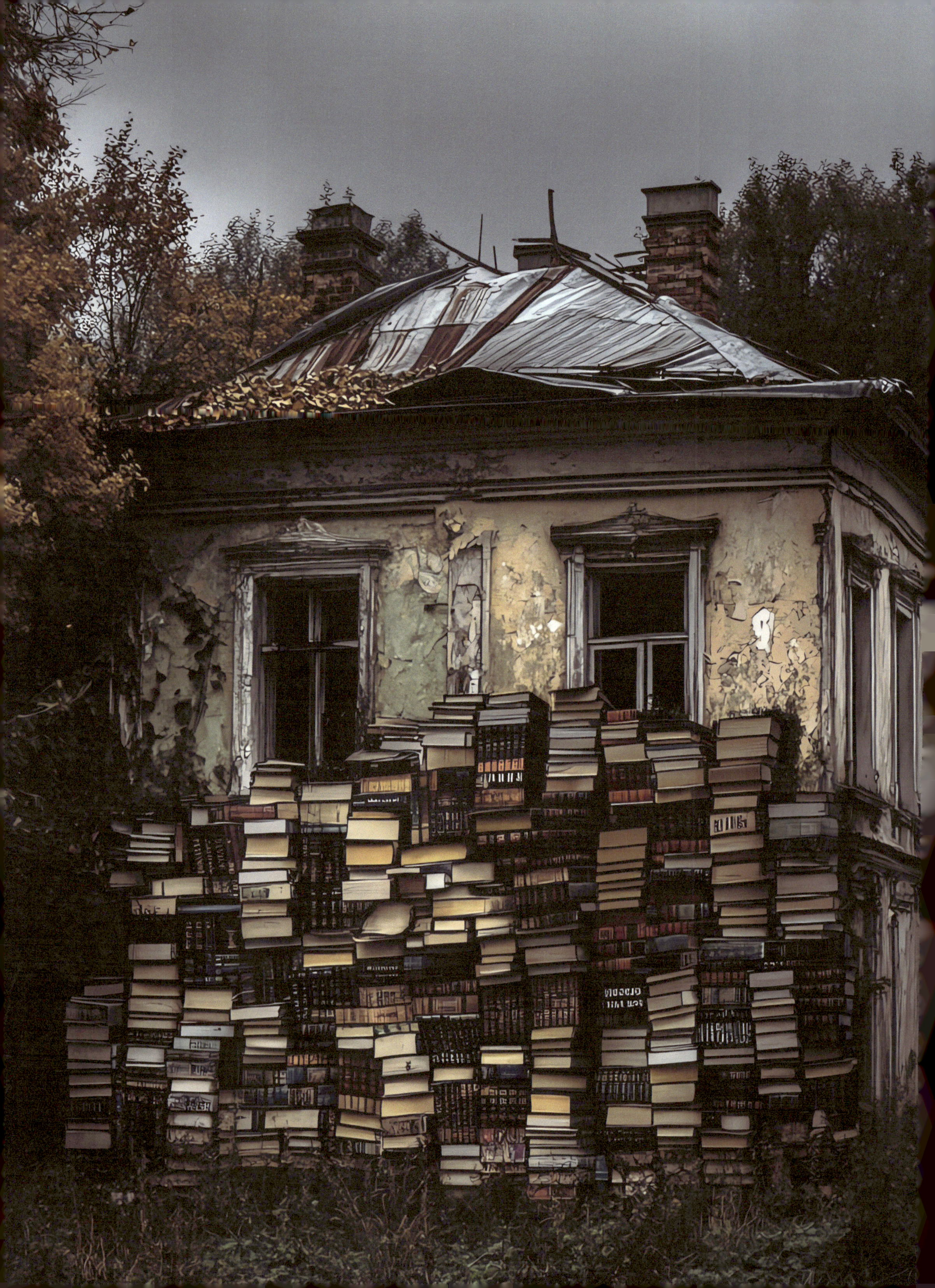